Faith-Based Reconciliation

Faith-Based Reconciliation

A Moral Vision That Transforms
People and Societies

Brian Cox

Library of Congress Control Number: 2007904720
ISBN: Hardcover   978-1-4257-7923-8
                  Softcover   978-1-4257-7908-5

This book was printed in the United States of America.

To order additional copies of this book, contact:
Xlibris Corporation
1-888-795-4274
www.Xlibris.com
Orders@Xlibris.com
38766

Contents

DEDICATION

To my wife, Ann who has loved and inspired me. She paid an enormous price with my absences from home over the past twenty five years.

To my children, Clare and John. It will be your generation that will bring the paradigm of faith-based reconciliation into its fullness.

To my mother, Mary who raised me to know and love God which would lead to my surrender to his will and the desire to serve him with my life.

Acknowledgements

This book would not be complete without acknowledging the many people that have brought it to fruition.

First, I would like to acknowledge my wife Ann and my children, Clare and John, without whose love, encouragement and sacrifice such an undertaking would never have been possible. They first believed in God's work of faith-based reconciliation through me.

Second, I would like to acknowledge the individuals who played a significant role as instruments of God in enabling me to catch the vision of faith-based reconciliation. This would include six longtime friends and colleagues: Frank Maguire, whose initiative in reaching out to Roman Catholics in Northern Ireland planted some early seeds within me; John Ashey, under whose pastoral leadership I matured into a servant leader with a heart for the nations; Bobb Biehl, my one time mentor who recognized and cultivated my gifts and leadership skills; Walter and Louise Hannum, whose vision and exhortation steered me eventually toward international reconciliation work; and Michael Harper, whose visionary statesmanship served as a model for me during my years with SOMA. My South African friends; Stephen Hayes, Dawn Leggat, Richard Kraft, Ben Photolo, Prince James Mahlangu and John Tooke were courageous instruments of reconciliation whose quiet efforts, among others, brought about the South African "miracle" and left an indelible mark on my life. I will also never forget the key role of Geza

Nemeth of Hungary who shared his vision for reconciliation in Europe with me one day in March 1990 in a living room in Budapest.

Third, I would like to acknowledge the individuals whose friendship, support or insights played significant roles in supporting this work or in shaping the foundations for the materials in this book. These would include Juraj Kohutiar, Konstantin Viktorin, Emil Komarik, and Anton Srholec of Slovakia; Zdenek Sedivy, and Josef Kubicek, from the Czech Republic; Peter Lucaciu of Romania; Dragan Dragojlovic of Serbia; Paul Toaspern and Christa Behr of Germany; Cecil Kerr of Northern Ireland; the Core Group from Indian Kashmir; Shah Qadir, Amjad Yousuf and the Core Group from Pakistani Kashmir; Michael Ahern, Oliver North, John Grinalds, Frank Salcedo, Herb Pearce, Tom Van Gorder, Gabe Joseph, Cindy Drennan, Craig Lyon, Tom Larkin, Alec Simpson, John Mumford, Vern Grose, Bill St. Cyr, Jack Morrill, Joanne O'Donnell, Doug Johnston, Dan Philpott, Carol Fay, Michael Witmer, and Doug Coe of the United States.

Fourth, I would like to acknowledge the many colleagues, associates and team members of the Reconciliation Institute, Reconcilers.Net and the International Center for Religion and Diplomacy who have contributed more than they will ever know. They have spent countless hours since Camp Whittier as agents of reconciliation through this work. My secretary, Leslie Smith, has spent hours on production of this manuscript.

Finally, I would like to thank the members of Christ the King Episcopal Church in Santa Barbara for their love, support, encouragement and participation in this work.

Chapter One

AN IDEA WHOSE TIME HAS COME

In March 1990, I made the first of over twenty trips to east Central Europe. As I drove with my two companions, Dr. Vernon Grose and Michael Ahern, across the heart of Central Europe from East Berlin to Bucharest, I encountered a region in chaos. Barely four months earlier, the Berlin Wall and the Iron Curtain, which had become powerful symbols of division and hostility between East and West, had been toppled by popular grassroots revolutionary movements. Religious leaders who had been the backbone of underground resistance movements were now beginning to emerge into the open. Intellectuals, who, only five months earlier, had been languishing in prison cells because of their opposition to the communist regimes were now serving as prime ministers and members of parliament. Ordinary people, who had suffered under an oppressive system, were now breathing the scent of genuine freedom for the first time in their lives. It was, indeed, a chaotic moment in history.

At the heart of the chaos that I encountered was the absence of any compelling moral vision for these societies. Over the course of the next eight years, I had conversations with hundreds of political and religious leaders as well as ordinary citizens. What began to emerge for me was an important insight about Marxism. For the people of East-Central Europe, Marxism had been more than an economic system. It had been a moral vision that for more than fifty years had shaped their political, social,

11

economic, cultural, and spiritual foundations. And now that moral vision was no more. But what was to come in its place? What was to fill the void? During those years, I witnessed three strong forces begin to emerge as alternative moral visions: nationalism, liberal democracy/free market capitalism, and militant Islam. In such places as Belgrade, Pale, and Zagreb former communists were reinventing themselves and becoming ardent nationalists. In such places as Prague, Bratislava, and Budapest, both Democratic and Republican political organizations based in Washington DC were actively promoting the unique blend of American liberal democracy and free market capitalism as a fresh moral vision. During the conflicts in Bosnia and Kosovo networks of Islamists from the Middle East, the Arabian Peninsula, Central Asia, and North Africa became involved with the Muslim communities and in the course of it shared their moral vision of global jihad.

In spite of my background in California electoral politics during the 1960s and 1970s, despite my years of theological training, it was in East-Central Europe during the chaotic period of the 1990s that for the first time in my life I began to understand the profound importance of moral vision in the life of individuals, societies, and nations. I also began to realize that, as a person of faith from the Abrahamic tradition, I was carrying in my heart the seed of an ancient moral vision, whose time on the world stage had finally come.

The French author Victor Hugo once wrote that there is nothing quite so powerful as an idea whose time has come. The world is not only shaped by people, events and interests, but also by ideas—soaring ideas that are not simply a reaction to the tectonic shifts of the geopolitical landscape but in themselves create new realities, new paradigms by providing the spiritual, social, political, and economic foundation for new societies and a new international order. These soaring ideas are moral vision.

The world or significant parts of it have been shaped by profound moral visions over the course of recorded history. I will briefly describe five moral visions that have defined a way of life or worldview over the past four millennia. In some ways, their influence has served the common good of humanity. They have inspired the noble side of human nature. In other ways, they have led to unforeseen consequences that have caused wars of conquest, deep divisions, hostility, conflict, violence, injustice, oppression, tyranny, totalitarianism, displaced peoples, poverty, hunger, ecological devastation, and wounded nations. These five moral visions are the Athenian democracy, the enlightenment secularism, the American experiment, the Marxist utopia, and the Abrahamic tradition.

Athenian Democracy

In the sixth century BCE, the social and political ferment of Athens and other Greek city-states gave birth to the concept of the polis as a community of free citizens and the novel concept of governance, which became known as democracy or rule by the consent of the governed. At the core of ancient democracy was the notion of citizenship, of belonging to a political society, which entailed both rights and responsibilities. While few of our modern understandings of liberal democracy can be traced back to these ancient roots, nevertheless, the basic notion of Athenian democracy represented a radical break from rule by monarchy or oligarchy, the normative expression of the time. This concept embodied a worldview, which eventually spread to the West and became embedded in Europe and, later, the United States. Today, that moral vision inspires nations and states all across the globe that are built on the core values of citizenship, rights, responsibilities, and the consent of the governed. As an American who grew up with these core values, I have often taken them for granted. I failed to appreciate the sacrifices made by my parents and so many in their generation who had to defend those core values against Nazi Germany and Imperial Japan. In October 1987, I was hosting a South African friend, Chris deBruyn, in our home in Northern Virginia. At one point as we were sitting together, he inhaled deeply and let out his breath slowly. When I asked him what he was doing, he replied, "I am learning what it is like to breathe the air of freedom." As a young colored man from South Africa, who had lived through some of the harshest years of the apartheid regime, he knew what it was to be a target of the Special Security Branch and to be the victim of a whole system of Afrikaner privilege. As an American, I had failed to appreciate how much the core values of Athenian democracy would mean to a young man from the continent of Africa.

Enlightenment Secularism

Beginning five hundred years ago, there were four key historical developments that profoundly shaped Europe's future and define contemporary geopolitical polarities, particularly between the West and the Islamic world. The first historical development was the Protestant Reformation, which ended the medieval synthesis and introduced the concept of separation of spiritual and temporal authority and contributed to the emergence of the state as an autonomous secular entity. The second historical development was the Peace of Westphalia, which brought an end to the Thirty Years' War (1618-1648). It established the principle of sovereignty that underlies relations between states to this day and which specified that no external power or deliberative body had the right to interfere in the domestic affairs of another state. The third historical development was the Enlightenment, which embodied the core value of human beings as the rational masters and unlimited sovereigns of their own fate. As such, it led to the development of a political and moral philosophy that embraced secular human reason rather than the sacred texts as the foundation for society. It also led to the concept of self-sovereignty of both the self and the state and removed the veil of accountability to a transcendent god. The fourth historical development was the French Revolution in 1789, which introduced the concept of popular sovereignty that the final authority in society is the will of the people. Hence, between the fifteenth and nineteenth centuries when Europe was experiencing both a religious reformation and a cultural renaissance, it was also undergoing a process of secularization.

Today, that moral vision is most deeply embodied in Western Europe and, to a lesser extent, the United States. In Western Europe, particularly, one witnesses the almost total absence of faith and religion from the public square and from the arena of policy making. The Christian faith—which formed the spiritual, philosophical and cultural soul of Europe—has virtually disappeared from the landscape. There is a growing presence of Muslims in Europe, but it is a minority and is viewed as an alien presence on European soil. The situation in the United States vis-à-vis secularism is far more complex. Many Europeans describe America as a nation with "the soul of a church." In other words, secularism is a major force in the American culture, but so too is religion, particularly Christianity and Judaism. While America might practice the core value of separation of church and state, it does not mean the absence of faith and religion from the public square. In fact, for many years, there has been a heated public conversation under way about the proper role and influence of religion in governance, policymaking, and politics.

Until September 11, 2001, it was normal for European and American secularists to dismiss religion as a significant factor in international politics. Religious actors such as Ayatollah Khomeini, whose ideology and activities stemmed from a spiritual or religious impulse, were often viewed as using religion as a guise for purely political or economic motives. This led to seriously flawed diagnoses and policies. However, since 9/11 all that has changed, since religion has emerged as a major force seeking to shape contemporary geopolitics. No policy maker in Europe or America can afford to ignore the role of religion as it intersects with politics and diplomacy. Given the growing estrangement between the Islamic world and the West (particularly the United States), it would seem that people of faith are in the best position to understand and build bridges to the Islamic world.

In February 2003, the International Center for Religion and Diplomacy (ICRD) hosted a group of Muslim political and religious leaders from Kashmir and Sudan at the National Prayer Breakfast in Washington DC. Given the stereotypical images they held about the United States as a secular nation, it came as a pleasant surprise for them to hear U.S. leaders talking about God, faith, and prayer. They heard Jewish, Christian, and even Muslim leaders speak about the need for a leadership under God, a leadership guided by spiritual and moral values. Toward the end of their visit, one senior Sudanese leader said, "I am going home with a very different and more complex view of America. I am also going home with a greater sense of hope that shared spiritual values can point the way forward in the future."

The American Experiment

The eighteenth century gave birth to a radically new vision of nation building that grew out of the experience of oppression and intolerance in Europe. The declaration of independence and the constitution of the United States envisioned a more perfect union that was later described as a shining city on a hill. The American experiment was built on the core values of radical individualism, freedom, justice, human rights, religious tolerance, separation of church and state, the rule of law, checks and balances, and economic opportunity. In a sense, it was a unique blending of liberal democracy with free market capitalism.

Today, that moral vision inspires nations that seek to emulate the American model such as Poland, the Czech Republic, or Hungary. It also inspires individuals and families that have immigrated to America because it represented opportunity that was lacking in their own nation. During a March 2005 visit to Ramallah in the Palestinian authority, I was speaking at a local church. During the service, I looked out over the small congregation and observed that there were very few people under the age of forty. After the worship service, I asked the pastor about this. He told me that young Palestinian Christians saw no future for themselves in the land. Between the Israeli policies experienced as oppressive by Palestinians and the growing influence of the Islamists, young Christians were feeling marginalized. He told me that many young Palestinian Christians had immigrated to Europe, but most had gone to America, where there was greater social and economic opportunity.

The Marxist Utopia

In the nineteenth century, a German philosopher put to pen his moral vision of a world that would be based on social justice and the emergence of governance by the proletariat. At the heart of that vision was an economic system based on collectivism and state socialism. Karl Marx wrote *Das Kapital,* whose principles were embraced by a Russian who became known as Lenin (man of steel). In the wake of the Russian Revolution, Lenin introduced Marxism into what became known as the Soviet Union. Marxism embodied a specifically atheistic view of the world and sought to create a classless society and the new "soviet man." Hence, the Marxist utopia was built on the core values of atheism, collectivism, state socialism, rule by the proletariat, and a classless society. Marxism lasted seventy-two years before popular revolution throughout the former Eastern Bloc led to its collapse as a viable system. However, much of the twentieth century was shaped by the moral vision of Karl Marx.

Today, that moral vision still inspires a few leaders in east Central Europe, who believe that the failure of the communist system had more to do with the greed of the leadership than any inherent flaw in its philosophical suppositions. In spring1993, I was part of a dinner and dialogue in Prague with the leadership of the Levy bloc of the Czech Republic. I sat directly across the dinner table from their leader, a formidable woman who had been the Levy bloc candidate for president against Vaclav Havel. At one point, the subject of the conversation turned to the nature of reconciliation in the Czech Republic. I was asked how I felt the Levy bloc could contribute to the process of reconciliation. I stated that they could begin by publicly acknowledging the sins of the past and apologizing to the Czech people. I was told that such an idea was not possible since the mistakes were the responsibility of the individuals in power rather than a flaw in the system.

For the most part the strongest adherents to the Marxist moral vision have been the proponents of liberation theology in Latin America. Inspired by the writings of Gustavo Gutierrez Merino and Leonardo Boff, this theology seeks to integrate Christianity and Marxism in adapting Marxist philosophy to the plight of the poor in Latin America by developing the concept of God's preferential option for the poor into forms of advocacy for social justice.

The Abrahamic Tradition

In Genesis 12:1-2, the Jewish scriptures tell of a revelation to Abraham in which God calls him forth from the security of family relationships, homeland, and collective identity to begin a new experiment which

16

ultimately will become known as *tikkun olam*—to heal, to repair, and to transform the world. As he journeys across the Fertile Crescent, Abraham holds in his bosom the kernel of a transcendent vision. He responds in faith and it germinates into what has become the Abrahamic tradition. Three great communities of faith, over three billion people, trace their roots back to this decisive revelation. The Davidic star, the cross, and the crescent—all are symbols that share in this defining moral vision. The Jewish scriptures relate how the Abrahamic tradition was further defined in a revelation to Moses—whom, with the liberated Hebrew slaves, God gives a covenant and moral law. It became the basis for a new society to be formed in the wilderness. The Torah was to be the core of a moral vision for society. It formed the basis of cultural values, institutions, and presuppositions within the new society that became known as Israel.

Two thousand years ago, when Jesus of Nazareth emerged upon the scene as a healer and reconciler, his simple message focused on the breaking in of the Kingdom of God or the establishment of God's new society on earth. This moral vision was grounded in the Abrahamic tradition, but he sought to universalize it for all peoples.

Through the life, teachings and example of Jesus, the Abrahamic tradition became further refined and crystallized. In my work of faith-based diplomacy, I summarize the ethical implications of this tradition in eight core values.

1. The pluralistic vision of community: we seek unity in the midst of diversity.
2. Compassionate inclusion: we seek to overcome hostility by the practice of unconditional love toward others, including one's enemies.
3. Peacemaking: we seek the peaceful resolution of conflicts between individuals and groups.
4. Social justice: we seek the common good through transformation of the soul of a community.
5. Forgiveness: we exercise forgiveness and repentance as individuals and communities to create the possibility of a better future together.
6. Healing: we seek to heal the wounds of history through acknowledgement of suffering and injustice.
7. Acknowledging God's sovereignty: We seek as individuals and communities to acknowledge God's authority through submission and surrender.
8. Atonement with God: We seek to find peace with God and become people of faith.

At the heart of these eight core values was the Abrahamic concept of God's sovereignty or rule over societies and nations. In the New Testament,

Jesus taught that God's sovereign rule would establish the common good, namely, a society based on respect for the dignity of every human being, the economics of compassion, the politics of love, the power of truth, and stewardship embodied in voluntary sacrifice. This was an ancient but radical moral vision in its day, and it still retains its revolutionary, transformational character in our day. It challenges people of faith in every age to a fundamental reorientation of their personhood and to the implementation of this vision in their societies. The apostle Paul called this radical moral vision as reconciliation.

Six hundred years later, a spiritual and social reform movement emerged from the sands of Arabia. Initially, Muhammed understood the revelations he received in Mecca and later Medina as a prophetic movement among Arab peoples. At the heart of his message and his mission was a reform movement that called Arabs to embrace the Abrahamic tradition of submission to the one true God (tawhid), adherence to a moral law revealed in the sacred texts (Sharia), and social justice as the basis for bringing about reconciled societies. More than any other tradition, Islam was grounded on a worldview characterized by the inseparable nature of faith and politics. They formed a seamless whole or a total way of life based on a unified worldview from the Qu'ran and the Sharia. In 622 CE, the community that had formed around Muhammed, and his teaching migrated to Yathrib (Medina), and there they sought to create a new society based on the religion of Abraham and on the transcendent values that the nascent Muslim community shared with the peoples of the book (Jews and Christians). Rising above Arab tribalism, Muhammed created an intentionally pluralistic and inclusive community grounded in social justice and forgiveness that sought to resolve conflict by peaceful means. He sought to heal the wounds of the past by forging a new Arab identity based on submission to God. Among contemporary Muslims, the Yathrib community of Muhammed's time serves as the paradigm or model for faith-based societies.

In September 2000, I made my first visit to Islamabad on behalf of the International Center for Religion and Diplomacy to explore the potential for ICRD's work on the Pakistani side of Kashmir. For the first time, I was meeting Islamic leaders and practicing Muslims in the context in which Islam was not only the state religion, but it also played a profound role in shaping Pakistani culture and identity. During the course of my visit, I found myself becoming preoccupied with one question, "What is the heart of the Islamic tradition which expresses its very soul?" I discovered my answer in a book given to me by its author, Dr. Jan Tarik, after our participation in a forum sponsored by the Institute for Policy Studies. In it, he described the heart of the Islamic faith as adherence to the Abrahamic tradition. As I sat in the quiet of my hotel room in Rawalpindi, a light went on in my soul. Suddenly, I realized the deep common bond shared by Jews, Christians, and Muslims. Each of us traced our spiritual roots back to Abraham as the quintessential man of faith, whose journey to the Promised Land modeled submission and surrender to the one true God. Each of us, in different ways, was grounded in the same fundamental core value of honoring and acknowledging the sovereignty of God over all life. Each of us had a sense of the Abrahamic family whether we called it Israel or the body of Christ or the *ummah*. Each of us shared in the gift of the Abrahamic homeland, a sacred land of promises and sorrows. Each of us shared in the Abrahamic mission to carry the blessing of *tikkun olam* or faith-based reconciliation to all the nations. Now, more than ever, our message and our mission are needed.

As we enter the twenty-first century, we have witnessed the collapse of the Marxist moral vision and the emergence of three major forces shaping the world: globalization, fragmentation, and religious fundamentalism. As globalization increases and with it the hegemony of hedonistic and secular values, we may be seeing the limits and logical consequences of the American experiment. As fragmentation causes societies to unravel and identity-based conflict to emerge, we may be seeing that Athenian democracy and the notion of citizenship are inadequate moral visions to address the powerful spiritual and social forces that are leading to a clash of civilizations. As religious fundamentalism arises as a counterpoint to Enlightenment secularism, we may be seeing the logical consequences of any moral vision that is not faith based that does not take into account the notion of divine sovereignty and the fundamental reality of spiritual hunger in the human soul. As we enter the twenty-first century, the time is ripe for us to revisit the Abrahamic tradition as a sweeping transcendent moral vision that, if implemented in the form of faith-based reconciliation, promises to be spiritual, social, political, and economic revolution in the affairs of nations.

This book will focus on eight core values that comprise a moral vision of faith-based reconciliation: pluralism, inclusion, peacemaking, social justice, forgiveness, healing wounds, sovereignty, and atonement. Each of these represents a principle. However, each forms the foundation for policy and program development that will heal and sustain societies. These eight core values are designed to be kept in dynamic tension with each other. They assume the centrality of relationships whether between two individuals or two nations. They assume a dynamic integration of transcendent faith with politics without imposing a particular sectarian or institutional perspective. They assume that religion has the potential to be both a source of conflict and an asset for peacemaking. They assume that reconciliation is not merely a response to a crisis or conflict; it is intended to be a permanent moral vision. Hence, it is the basic message of this book that the Abrahamic tradition embodied as faith-based reconciliation is an idea whose time has come.

Chapter Two

RECONCILIATION AND COLLECTIVE IDENTITY

Collective identity is a complex matrix of constituent elements such as gender, ethnicity, language, homeland, citizenship, religion, culture, social class, region, political ideology, suffering, injustice, or exile that defines the distinctiveness of a people group, creates its soul, and shapes its interests, strategic alliances, and antagonisms.

In July 2002, over fifty Kashmiri Muslims and Hindu pandits gathered at a hotel in the small mountainous village of Gulmarg, three miles inside the Indian side of the Line of Control. The atmosphere was filled with anxiety, uncertainty and tension. Thirteen years earlier, some 400,000 Kashmiri pandits had fled the Kashmir Valley. Pandits claimed that they were driven out of the valley by Muslims. The Muslims claimed that the exodus was engineered by the Indian government. Nevertheless, most pandits ended up in squalid refugee camps near Jammu, living in a context of fear and hopelessness. For the twenty-six Kashmiri pandits, who had come for the faith-based reconciliation seminar, it was their first time returning to the Kashmir Valley. It was a predictably emotional time for them. On the first evening, I sat and listened as a dozen pandits shared with me about their sense of loss and suffering. Their hostility toward Muslims was not even subtle. As I listened to their pejorative description of Muslims, I had an ominous feeling in the pit of my stomach. I knew that the next three days were going to be very painful. Both Kashmiri Muslims and pandits shared a deep identity and passion for Kashmir—its land, its culture, and its language. They were Kashmiris! And yet as we gathered that first evening there was a clear sense of "us" and "them" defined by religious differences. As I witnessed so vividly that night, religion played an integral role in the politics of identity.

In many respects, both national and international politics of the twenty-first century have become the politics of identity. This implies that cross-cultural differences serve as a primary factor in conflict. Theologian Miroslav Volf wrote in his book *Exclusion and Embrace*, "Might not the will for identity be fueling a good deal of those fifty or so conflicts around the globe. Various kinds of cultural cleansings demand of us to place identity and otherness at the center of theological discussion." This important theological insight was also captured and expressed in the strategic political realm by political scientist Samuel Huntington in a 1993 summer article in *Foreign Affairs* journal. Huntington used the metaphor "clash of civilizations" in an effort to describe an emerging post-Cold War world order and the importance of ethnicity, culture, and religion in a dramatic reconfiguration of global politics.

The metaphor "clash of civilizations" has been one of the most thought provoking, oft-quoted, and controversial strategic concepts to emerge in the realm of diplomacy and international politics in the last fifty years. It is particularly controversial in the Islamic world, which is described by Huntington as having "bloody borders." Regardless of its controversial nature, "clash of civilizations" cannot be summarily dismissed. It merits probing and pondering to understand its implications in twenty-first century geopolitics. As such, this strategic concept needs to be understood at a more profound level, particularly in terms of its relationship to a moral vision of faith-based reconciliation. What does it mean?

First, the clash of civilizations means that collective identity is a primary factor in shaping interests, strategic alliances, and antagonisms in national and international politics. The tenth chapter of the Book of Genesis in the Jewish scriptures would seem to suggest that collective identity and distinctiveness is, and always has been, part of God's plan for creation to provide a source of human dignity and belonging. In that chapter, we witness the birth of collective identity in the table of nations derived from the sons of Noah. The Qu'ran also teaches the positive nature of collective identity and encourages a level of striving in good deeds toward "the other" (Surah 5:48).

The formation of collective identity is an intriguing subject discussed by psychologist Robert Coles in his book, *The Political Life of Children.* His study sought to answer the fundamental question, "How do children come to see themselves in terms of ethnic, cultural, or religious identity?"

Shaping by parents, educational, religious, and social institutions play a significant role in the formation of our collective identity. These shaping institutions, which exist in every culture, create in each one of us a sense of distinctiveness, of group identity, of "us," and of "them." They create our worldview, our sense of core values, our loyalties, our aspirations, our interests, and our prejudices and antagonisms. In a sense, they create the very soul of an identity-based group.

In most cases, until threatened, collective identity is benign and passive in its definition of a people group. However, depending on local, regional, national, or international events at a particular time, one or more aspects of our collective identity might emerge as defining factors in shaping political interests, strategic alliances, or antagonisms. Often, such distinctions are invoked by demagogues bent on inflaming conflict. In other words, our ethnic identity or our religious identity or our political ideology might become lightening rods for conflict with "the other." In terms of faith-based reconciliation, it means that true and full reconciliation cannot take place without the will to embrace "the other."

I am a middle-age white male of European (German/French) descent born in Chicago, Illinois, but lived most of my life in Southern California. I am a child of Abraham and a follower of Jesus from the Anglican-Christian tradition. In terms of political ideology, I would define myself as a bridge-building conservative. I have traveled to every region of the United States and overseas to some seventy-eight countries. At one point or another, I have found that each part of my collective identity has played a role in defining me as "the other." However, if I am honest with myself, I must admit that collective identity plays a role in how I define "the other." On one occasion some years ago, I arrived for a community meeting in my hometown of Santa Barbara. As I found a place at the table and surveyed the other participants and listened to the concerns on their hearts, it occurred to me that I represented the other to every single person sitting at that table.

Second, the "clash of civilizations" means that in many cases, religion serves as the anchor point in collective identity. Perhaps the most neglected and unappreciated aspect of diplomacy and policy making is the spiritual and religious dimension. Such activities as prayer, trust in God, sacred texts, forgiveness, or repentance rarely, if ever, find their way into traditional diplomatic discourse or Western secular conflict resolution models. Rarely, if ever, is God's role in changing human hearts acknowledged by secular practitioners of bridge building, conflict resolution, or social justice. Transformation is often seen as simply self-actualization of the human potential or as individuals acting in their own best interest or even more cynically as impossible.

In the *Illustrated Dictionary of Religions,* Philip Wilkinson defines religion thus:

> A religion is a set of beliefs and practices, often associated with a supernatural power that shapes or directs human life and death, or a commitment to ideas that provide coherence for one's existence. Adherence to a religion implies a belief in a divine force, as well as offering moral guidance for believers. Religions also bind people into communities with common goals and values.

Religion reflects the reality of spiritual hunger within the human soul and the need to find peace with God, self, and others. Historian Scott Appleby defines four constituent elements of religion. The first is a *creed,* which defines the standard of beliefs concerning the ultimate origin, meaning, and purpose of life. This is generally a body of ideas and teachings called doctrines or dogma. It might also refer to a short confessional statement taken as a first step of conversion and faith. The second is a *cultic expression*—which encompasses the prayers, devotions, spiritual disciplines, communal worship and ritual, holy days and seasons, sacred places, religious institutions and sacred objects, and icons. The third is a *moral code* that defines explicit behavioral norms as well as a fundamental moral vision for the larger society. The fourth is a *confessional community,* which defines personal and social identity and which provides a supportive context for spiritual growth.

In spring 1995, my friend, Juraj Kohutiar, and I traveled to Sarajevo, Bosnia, for the first time. As we met with different Bosnian religious leaders—such as the grand mufti, the Roman Catholic cardinal, and the Serbian Orthodox Metropolitan—we found that they shared a great deal in common in their love for Bosnia and their genuine heartache over the conflict. Nevertheless, it was their religious identity that served as the anchor point of their collective identity and defined the contours of the conflict. While it was not and never was a religious conflict, still religion formed the basis of communal identity.

Third, the clash of civilizations means that ethnicity, religion, and culture will serve as catalysts in provoking intractable identity-based conflict. We might define culture in the following manner:

> Culture embodies both the worldviews and values of a people as well as the outward manifestation in their common life, and, in the face, they present to the global community.

Thus, there is an intangible dimension to culture, which embodies the worldviews and values of a particular community or society. How do they view reality? How do they attach meaning and significance to their existence? What are their core values? How do they understand and interpret their history? How do they see themselves in relationship to other people groups? What is their understanding of ultimate reality or the divine?

There is also a tangible dimension to culture, which embodies the outward manifestations of a people group's way of life. What is the individual's relationship to the group? How are decisions made for the group? What is the nature of gender relationships? How do they define public and private space? What are considered appropriate and acceptable social patterns? Is the group hierarchical or egalitarian? How and to whom is respect shown in their culture? What is the nature of their music and literature?

As a lifelong Anglican, I went through a period during my young adult years when I was profoundly shaped by the evangelical culture within Christianity. This included a worldview of winning the world to Christ, which usually meant sharing the gospel message about Jesus with a non-Christian, leading them to commit their life to Jesus as their Savior and Lord, making a complete break from their religious tradition, and embracing a particular cultural and institutional expression of Christianity. Hence, from an evangelical perspective or worldview, the Muslim world was lost and needed to be won for Christ. It was not until I visited a Dawa Academy in Islamabad in 2000 and spoke with the director general that I realized that the same worldview was prevalent in the Muslim world in the opposite direction, wherein Christians were viewed as kaffirs or infidels. In his academy, young Muslims were shaped by a worldview of extending dar al-Islam—which usually meant rule by Islamic leaders and institutions with Christians, Jews, and others being granted dhimmi status as protected minorities. Two worldviews shaped by religion guaranteeing a permanent state of hostility and defining a conflict that has lasted almost fourteen hundred years. An intractable conflict by anybody's definition.

Fourth, the clash of civilizations means that the traditional models of conflict resolution are inadequate to address most intractable identity-based conflicts. Hence, a new paradigm is needed. That paradigm is faith-based reconciliation. The word "reconciliation" is a powerful word in any language that frequently engages deep emotions and passions in people. It is also an ancient word with roots that go back at least four thousand years. The Hebrew derivatives are the expressions *tikkun olam* and *shalom*. *Tikkun olam* means "to heal, to repair, and to transform the world." In other words, over time the ancient Hebrews began to understand that God's basic purpose

25

for creation was to heal, to restore, and to transform. At the heart of the Abrahamic tradition is this sense of divine purpose. The goal of *tikkun olam* is *shalom*, which means "wholeness, harmony, and integrity." *Shalom* means reconciliation with God, self, and others. The Greek derivatives from the New Testament are the words *katallage, apokatallasso,* and *diallasso. Katallage* means "to bring forces together that would naturally repel each other" such as the two positive ends of a magnet. *Apokatallasso* means "to break down walls or barriers," such as those that might exist between two estranged or hostile groups. *Diallasso* means "to heal or change the nature of a relationship" through a process of truth telling, repentance, and forgiveness. The Latin derivative from the Roman tradition is the word *concilium,* which means a deliberative process in which conflicting partners meet each other in council to work out their differing views and to arrive at some common agreement. The Arabic derivatives are the words *salima* and *salaha. Salima* means "to establish peace, safety, security, and freedom." *Salaha* or *sulh* means "settlement, reconciliation, peacemaking, and restoration." The Sanskrit derivatives are the words *dhynan* (Zen) and *yoga. Dhynan* means "awakening or enlightenment" leading to liberation, reconciliation, atonement, and submission to the divine. *Yoga* means "union or integration."

In July 2005, a group of youth from my congregation made a spiritual pilgrimage to England and Ireland to explore their relationship with God, their Anglican roots, and God's work of reconciliation. In their report upon their return, I was struck by their observations about their time in Belfast concerning the deep hostility and estrangement that still exists between Protestant and Catholic youth. In spite of the Good Friday Accord of 1998, the hostility and conflict is still carried on in hearts that have not yet been transformed.

Reconciliation is a rich and complex concept that cannot be captured and expressed by any single definition. Rather, it is like the facets of a diamond that each reflects only a portion of the totality. However, at the heart of faith-based reconciliation is restored relationships with God, self, and others. As such, reconciliation is both a spiritual and a political word that speaks of the centrality of personal relationships so that what is true for individuals also applies to communities and nations.

Collective identity, religion, and culture form the matrix of an international system based on the clash of civilizations. Faith-based reconciliation represents a moral vision or paradigm for shaping that international system. We now turn our attention to a consideration of each of the eight core values of that moral vision.

Chapter Three

BUILDING BRIDGES
THE PRINCIPLE OF PLURALISM

Pluralism means that we seek unity in the midst of diversity.

In 1998, the Lambeth Conference comprising Anglican bishops from the worldwide Anglican Communion overwhelmingly passed a resolution reaffirming the Anglican Church's traditional teaching on human sexuality. This came as a shock to the members of the gay and lesbian community within the Episcopal Diocese of Los Angeles, who had actually dared to believe the sign in front of many Episcopal Churches that reads, "The Episcopal Church welcomes you." The community met in September with the diocesan bishops to vocalize their feelings of anger and marginalization. However, two participants in the meeting, Joanne O'Donnell and Michael Witmer, decided to take some positive action by discovering why conservatives in the diocese felt the way they did. At the Diocesan convention in December, O'Donnell and Witmer had an encounter with members of a conservative advocacy group, the American Anglican Council, and together they decided to begin a dialogue. It became an important first step of building bridges in a highly conflicted religious community. A few people of faith were willing to chance the arm and undertake the painful diplomatic work of exploring the meaning and boundaries of a pluralistic community among Anglicans in Southern California.

E Pluribus Unum, "out of many . . . one." Pluralism can have two meanings. The first is existential pluralism which is the simple fact that diverse peoples exist in a given area, society, or organization. These entities are multiethnic, interreligious, or otherwise diverse—which are manifested in such cosmopolitan cities such as Los Angeles, Toronto, London, or Jerusalem. In other words, existential pluralism does not imply any principle. It is merely descriptive.

However, pluralism is also a principle or core value about how we ought to regard the existence of diverse entities in a given area, society, or organization. Pluralism, as a principle, begins with the belief that differences in language, ethnicity, gender, and many aspects of culture are, in and of themselves, something valuable. From the perspective of faith-based reconciliation, such differences are created by God or by humans creating as God has enabled them; they thus reflect the manifold glory of God's creation. The Torah, for instance, makes clear that God created humans into male and female and into nations.

The Qu'ran, as well, affirms diversity as part of God's purpose in creation. As it is written in Surah 49:13, "O mankind! We created you from a single pair of a male and a female, and made you into nations and tribes, that ye may know each other, not that ye may despise each other. Verily, the most honored of you in the sight of Allah is he who is the most righteous of you. And Allah has full knowledge and is well acquainted with all things." In the New Testament, the outpouring of the Holy Spirit at the time of Pentecost enabled people of diverse languages to understand one another. However, they retained their distinctive tongues, they manifested their diversity, but it was no longer a barrier that created enmity. Hence, in God's created order, humans fruitfully manifest variegated languages, architecture, music, dance, literature, technology, and political and economic organization.

Nevertheless, the beauty of differences is expressed not just in their isolation but also in communication, interaction, and relationship. The principle of pluralism deepens in recognition that greater wholeness, an even more enhanced beauty, is achieved when different people and communities come together and share their knowledge and goodwill. Humans are fulfilled only in association when people bring diverse gifts into the context of that association. I live in the community of Santa Barbara, which, for its size, is incredibly diverse. The Latino population is officially between 30 and 35 percent. There is also a small African American community, Chinese, Japanese, Korean, Vietnamese, Cambodian, German, Irish, Russian, Ukrainian, and Greeks. In spite of the fact that Anglos and Latinos share the same postal zip codes, there is little meaningful interaction between them. It is an example that is true of so many communities where there is existential pluralism but an absence of principled pluralism.

Pluralism, as a principle, means that we show respect for distinctions while we focus on the basis for common ground. In other words, pluralism is grounded in a respect for the dignity of every human being. The common good flows from the understanding that all human beings are created in the image or attributes of God and are, therefore, worthy of respect. Respect is a foundation of justice and, hence, part of what Aristotle defined as "our due," what human beings owe to each other. Consider the Ten Commandments given to Moses and Israel. These were the essence or core of a moral law and can be summarized in one word: respect. At the heart of what human beings owe to each other is respect for one another's personhood. For three years, I participated in a small group of Santa Barbara pastors called Pastors Pursuing Racial Reconciliation. On one occasion, we were talking about how we dress on our one-day off each week. Most of the Anglo pastors shared that they dressed very casually, and some even neglected to shave. However, the African American pastors shared with us that if they went outside the house, they would always wear a coat and tie; otherwise, they would not be treated with respect by many of the merchants in the community. As Anglos, we subconsciously took for granted that we should be treated with respect regardless of how we were dressed. Our African American colleagues were opening our eyes to a reality of their world—that they could not take for granted the expectation of being treated with respect.

Pluralism as a principle requires the defining of a common ground, a common set of core values. Common ground itself is defined by a sense of shared values that transcend the distinctiveness of constituent elements of a society. When common ground is defined on the basis of ethnicity, culture, or religious tradition, it inherently leads not to unity but to uniformity, balkanization, or tribalism. Hence, shared core values is the true foundation of pluralism. "To be Pakistani is to be Muslim, so where does that leave us as a Christian community, who take pride in our Pakistani identity and culture but in many ways feel that we don't belong?" Such was the cry that I heard so many times during a visit I made to the Diocese of Faisalabad in 1999. The use of institutional religious identity as a basis for unity had left, at least one community, feeling alienated and excluded. In 2004, I attended the annual convention of the Islamic Society of North America in Chicago at the invitation of Dr. Sayed Sayeed. I heard that same cry from American Muslims who viewed themselves as loyal American citizens but wondered if there was a place for them at the table because of their Islamic identity.

Pluralism as a principle also means that diversity has its limits, which must be defined by every society in terms of the range of tolerable deviation from the norm. No society can embrace unlimited diversity. Nor should it. Not all diversity is redemptive or even an expression of the noble character of human nature. While racism, for example, might lurk in the human heart, should it be embraced as an acceptable aspect of diversity? This, of course, raises a fundamental tension between the expression of individual freedom and the need to subordinate the rights of the individual to the common good of the society. At what point does the deviation from the norm become antisocial or destructive to communal harmony? How are the limits to diversity established, enforced, and adjusted? How does this relate to being a free and open society as opposed to an authoritarian and closed society? Britain is a nation that has prided itself in its embrace of multiethnic and multicultural expressions as an evolving part of British identity. However, in the wake of the July 2005 London bombings, many political leaders began to ask the question whether or not Britain could continue to tolerate unlimited diversity by allowing violent forms of militant Islam to exist in its society. Were the fiery sermons and militant network of the North Central London Mosque an acceptable part of British diversity?

Jesus of Nazareth taught the principle of pluralism in his choice of disciples and followers. One of his disciples was a man by the name of Simon the Zealot. Simon was an ardent Jewish nationalist. In the context of the Roman occupation, he detested their presence and associated himself with a movement to foment political revolution and Jewish independence. At the same time, Jesus invited a man named Matthew to be one of his followers. Matthew was a tax collector, who made his living from cooperation with the Roman authorities. Two men, two political worldviews, that Jesus called into association and told them they were going to learn to love each other—an intentional pluralistic society.

For pluralism to move from being merely descriptive to being a principle or core value, there must be an intentionality of action through the building of bridges. Bridge building means developing the tangible and intangible strands of connectedness among diverse people groups, in a community or state, so that they can live together in peace and seek the common good of the whole community. Bridge building reflects the fact that reconciliation systems have an identifiable architecture for knotting together the diverse elements of a modern society.

Bridges have inspired poets, novelists, artists, and photographers through the ages. They bring together two pieces of geography, sometimes two worlds that otherwise might not come together and be enriched by each other. The construction of a bridge begins at both ends and, finally, meets in the middle of a span. Building bridges is an apt metaphor in the area of human relationships, whether between two individuals or two nations, and it is absolutely essential in order to forge unity out of diversity. Thus, a pluralistic society or state is predicated upon a proactive effort to build bridges.

The architecture of bridge building develops in discreet stages. *Social bridge building* focuses on relationships. It deals with feelings, attitudes, opinions, and perceptions and is a means to engendering a new social fabric through activities such as dialogues, exchanges, and community-building activities. Over the years, I have participated in numerous dialogues. Each has been awkward; at times joyous; and, at other times, frustrating, painful, or superficial. Yet each was valuable in beginning to build a bridge to people who were "the other." Such was true as a small group of us organized an initiative within the national Episcopal Church to bring together theological conservatives, moderates, and liberals to have a conversation about the issues surrounding human sexuality. We called this initiative the New Commandment Task Force. *Spiritual bridge building* focuses on beliefs and values. It deals with creeds, rituals, customs, and morals as they are held and shared between individuals or groups through such activities as sharing life/spiritual journeys, study groups, and pilgrimages. For two years, my friend, Rabbi Richard Shapiro, and I led a study group of Episcopalians and Reformed Jews as we focused on Abraham in the Book of Genesis. I personally experienced it as a rich time of better understanding the deep faith of our Jewish cousins in the Abrahamic family. *Political bridge building* focuses on forging agreements. It deals with establishing political arrangements that enable diverse people groups to understand the basis and boundaries for living together. These might include peace accords or treaties. On one occasion, I was participating in a breakfast meeting that the mayor of Santa Barbara had hosted for Latino religious leaders. When asked by the mayor what reconciliation would look like to them, one Roman Catholic priest responded, "Regardless of all your kind words, we, who are Latinos, still know that at the end of the day, it is still the white guys that pull the levers of power in this community. When we see that change, then we will begin to believe in reconciliation." *Structural bridge building* focuses on activities. It deals with creating structure and institutions that enable diverse people groups to interact with each other—such as political, economic, and social infrastructures. One of the contributions that the International Center for Religion and Diplomacy has made in the conflict in Sudan has been through the efforts of my colleague, Dr. Douglas Johnston, to establish an interreligious council, which brings representatives from both Muslim and Christian communities together to create opportunities and deal with problems between the two religious communities.

There is a catalogue of destructive forces that bridge builders have to overcome or transform in modern societies. The need for bridge building seems to result from the ever-diminishing ability of different communities to live independently or in isolation because of the forces of globalization. There are a variety of human situations that cry out for the need for bridge building. One of these is where two social, ethnic, or religious groups live in proximity to each other but have no historical or preexisting relationship. Simply because two identity-based groups that live in geographical proximity to each other does not mean that there is any meaningful interaction, any sense of shared community, or any commitment to the common good. In a sense, they are living in isolation from each other, which can lead to a perception of "us" vs. "them." Perhaps this can even cause people groups to misunderstand, fear, or mistrust each other. Frequently, certain cultural or group behaviors can be offensive to the other group, which can lead to hostility, conflict, or political atomization. It takes great courage sometimes for the bridge builder to cross the wall of silence and establish relationship and trust with "the other." In the postmortem analysis of the Los Angeles riots in 1992, it was discovered, to the surprise of many, that tensions between African Americans and Korean merchants had been a significant contributing factor in the riots. In a sense, two communities lived side by side but had little meaningful interaction between them.

A second situation is where there are irreconcilable viewpoints. In every community, there may be certain political or public policy issues that strongly polarize its citizens. Or there might be certain religious beliefs and values which cause offense to outside groups. It is human nature to personalize the political issue or offending religious belief, which leads to demonization of the group. Irreconcilable viewpoints usually arise out of two processes. People may weigh the same evidence and arrive at different conclusions, or they may begin from two completely different basic premises. Nevertheless, the outcome is the same. Viewpoints on issues can lead to hostility, conflict, or demonization. Bridge builders enable political opponents or competing religious groups to meet each other as people in spite of their profound differences. I think of the quiet efforts in our community of two courageous bridge builders who have sought to bring together pro-choice and pro-life advocates to lower the walls of hostility between those two political advocacy groups.

A third situation is where there are personality clashes. Sometimes identity-based groups are estranged from each other because leaders of the two groups dislike each other on a personal level or annoy and offend each other. Hence, personality clashes between leaders can filter down to the popular level leading to wholesale demonization. Bridge builders enable two leaders who personally dislike each other to discover each other at a deeper or more profound level, which can transform the antagonism into friendship. During my second trip to Ladakh in 2004, I was surprised to discover that at one time in the past tensions between the Buddhist and Muslim communities in Leh began when the leader of one community publicly slapped the face of a leader from the other community. Their personal clash soon spread through both communities.

A fourth situation is where there is inherited or acquired prejudice. Prejudice is a preformed opinion based on ignorance—which focuses on race, nationality, culture, appearance, values, and tastes. Prejudice is universal and is often inherited from family, societal stereotypes, or painful experiences with other people groups. Bridge builders enable members of different social or religious groups to face up to their prejudices and discover friendship and common ground. In October 1990, I was serving at Church of the Apostles in Fairfax, Virginia, when we hosted eight religious leaders from East Germany, Czechoslovakia, Hungary, and Romania. Each came from a religious tradition that held certain suspicions or prejudices about the others. I know that our efforts were bearing fruit when, during a break in one of our meetings, a leader from the Conservative Brethren Church of Romania pointed to the rosary of a Dominican Catholic monk from Prague and asked, "How does that work?"

The fifth situation is where there are two or more parties actively engaged in a conflict wherein bridge building in its various forms would provide the architecture for third party intervention with an eye toward getting the conflicting parties to the negotiating table. In the realm of conflict resolution, this is known as caucusing with the parties. In the world of international affairs, it is known as shuttle diplomacy. Professionals in conflict resolution keep an eye open for people known as linking pins, often middle-level leaders who have the flexibility not available to senior-level leaders to entertain and pursue risky and creative initiatives in conflict situations. This is known as back channel diplomacy. Perhaps the best example of this was the work of the community of San Egidio in Mozambique, which employed the practice of gospel friendship in building trusting relationships with leaders from both Renamo and Frelimo, in the long-standing conflict. Eventually, their quiet bridge-building efforts brought both parties to the negotiating table.

Bridge builders are, in a sense, civic diplomats. Diplomacy, in its most restrictive sense, is generally associated with official relationships between nation-states. However, perhaps we need to rediscover its broader application as an interactive process between various parties that includes relationship building, communication of information, and negotiation. Can we imagine civic diplomats being raised up and encouraged by public officials on the local, regional, and national level and whose primary task would be to move among different communities and build bridges of friendship, trust, and understanding? Can we imagine track-two diplomats being recognized and encouraged by foreign ministries on the international level and whose primary task would be to build informal networks of relationships through civil society? As civic diplomats, bridge builders have the ability to move fruitfully among diverse communities to build relationship and establish trust. They have an appreciation and respect for different cultures—an ability to communicate across cultures, an ability to appreciate the complexities and subtle nuances of situations, an ability to form networks of people, to be an active listener, to ask pivotal questions, to be patient, to be persistent, and to persevere. Bridge builders are the diplomatic glue that is needed in every community and nation.

Besides quiet diplomacy, bridge builders are willing to "chance the arm." This is an expression that comes from a fifteenth-century incident involving two families, the Ormonds and the Kildares, who were part of the worshipping community of St. Patrick's Anglican Cathedral in Dublin, Ireland.

ST. PATRICK'S CATHEDRAL, DUBLIN

In 1492, two prominent families, the Ormonds and Kildares, were in the midst of a bitter feud. Besieged by Gerald Fitzgerald Earl of Kildare, Sir James Butler, Earl of Ormond and his followers took refuge in the chapter house of St. Patrick's Cathedral, bolting themselves in. As the siege wore on, the Earl of Kildare concluded that the feuding was foolish. Here were two families worshipping the same God, in the same church, living in the same country, trying to kill each other. So he called out to Sir James and, as an inscription in St. Patrick's says today, "undertook on his honour that he should receive no villanie".

Wary of "some further treacherie", Ormond did not respond. So Kildare seized his spear, cut away a hole in the door and thrust his hand through. It was grasped by another hand inside the church, the door was opened and the two men embraced, thus ending the family feud.

The expression "chancing one's arm" originated from Kildare's noble gesture. There is a lesson here for all of us who are engaged in "family feuds", whether brother to brother, language to language, nation to nation. If one of us would dare to "chance his arm", perhaps that would be the first crucial step to the reconciliation we all unconsciously seek.

At a certain point, the Earl of Kildare concluded that the feuding was foolish, and he was willing to risk having his arm cut off to bridge the gulf of estrangement with the Ormonds. Hence, "to chance the arm" means to be willing to take the first step to move across the chasm of alienation or conflict that might exist between families and communities. There is always the risk that one's initial overture will be rebuffed. There is always the risk of looking weak. There is always the risk of being misunderstood. Bridge builders are present in every community who have the vision and the courage to take the first step toward embracing a new possibility in a relationship or a conflict with another community, who carry the hope and see the need for reconciliation.

Besides quiet diplomacy and chancing the arm, bridge builders also value and utilize the tool of dialogue, which enables separated or estranged peoples to sit and talk with each other in a structured format and create political cover for leaders who might otherwise be reluctant to show movement. Dr. Louise Diamond, formerly of the Institute for Multi-Track Diplomacy, offers a number of insights about the dialogue process. She points out that dialogue is particularly essential with those whom we may think that we have the greatest differences. The purpose of dialogue is not to advocate, but to inquire; not to argue, but to explore; and not to convince, but to discover. Dialogue serves a very different purpose than debate. There is room in every society for debate about public policy issues that allow divergent points of view to be expressed and advocated. Debate empowers us to think through complex issues for ourselves and arrive at thoughtful conclusions. However, true dialogue seeks to create a safe space in a context of respect that allows individuals or groups to share their perspectives on difficult, controversial, or explosive issues. In a true dialogue, there is an implicit agreement that the purpose is learning and to deepen understanding of "the other." The simple structure of statement, reflection, and clarification can enable a truly respectful environment to exist between individuals or groups, where there is an existing or potential antagonism. Bridge builders are the enablers of dialogue that create deeper understanding between ethnic, social, or religious groups.

In conclusion, pluralism is the first core value of faith-based reconciliation, and the means to its implementation is bridge building.

Chapter Four

DEMOLISHING WALLS OF HOSTILITY
THE PRINCIPLE OF INCLUSION

Compassionate inclusion means that we seek to overcome hostility by the practice of unconditional love toward others, including one's enemies.

I grew up in a large conservative church in Whittier, California. I remember vividly the Sunday in 1965 when a young couple from the congregation came and spoke to my Sunday school class about their experience of marching with Dr. Martin Luther King Jr. from Selma to Montgomery, Alabama, in the cause of civil rights for African Americans. As a fifteen-year-old youth, I didn't know too much about the civil rights movement. However, as I listened to that couple share about their experience, there was something in my heart that stirred that day. Somehow, what they did seemed to me to be both courageous and an authentic expression of the Abrahamic tradition. I soon discovered, however, that many of the adults in the congregation did not share my reaction. I learned from overhearing my parents one night that there was talk going around the church that this couple were dangerous radicals, and it was even surmised that they were closet communists seeking to undermine God and country. Some months later, that poor couple, feeling distinctly unwelcome, left the church and joined the Quakers down the street.

In 1972, I left behind my conservative upbringing in Southern California to pursue my theological studies. I soon discovered that, both theologically and politically, I was not part of the mainstream of the community. On more than one occasion, I shared my feelings of being "out of synch" with the overwhelming majority of the community. I was quickly reassured that the community practiced radical inclusiveness. I didn't know exactly what "radical inclusiveness" meant, but, over the course of my three years there, I experienced a profound sense of loneliness and exclusion. Nevertheless, I could not escape the fact that the sacred texts clearly point to God's inclusive love for all people. As I have wrestled with this principle for the past fifteen years, I have discovered that the key to inclusion involves both distinct moral choices on how we relate to "the other" and also our willingness to confront our own hostility toward "the other."

In confronting people or groups who are different than ourselves in terms of ethnicity, class, culture, religion, or political ideology, there are three basic postures that involve distinct moral choices. The first posture is that of exclusion—where we judge "the other" to be offensive, undesirable, inferior, or evil, and we seek to drive them from our midst by means of social ostracism or isolation, economic injustice, or ethnic cleansing. The second posture is that of tolerance, where we judge "the other" with veiled but respectful indifference. We seek neither to exclude them nor to embrace them. They are "there" but they are "not there." Tolerance, to the casual observer, would appear to be an acceptable standard of group coexistence. Certainly, one could argue that tolerance is an improvement over the intolerance of the twentieth century. Some years ago, in a meeting with the president of the Jewish community of Slovakia, Dr. Pavel Traubner, he said, "Brian, we in the Jewish community are tired of simply being tolerated. In the end, I suppose that tolerance is better than the intolerance that we have known. However, just once, couldn't we be cherished for who we are?" Yet people of faith should be reminded that tolerance is not the standard of the sacred texts but rather the minimum standard of civility, which essentially concedes the darker side of human nature. The third posture is that of embrace, where we judge "the other" to be worthy of respectful engagement, and we seek to enter their world even if it causes a significant level of angst within our own being. This posture of embrace is at the heart of inclusion, the second principle or core value of faith-based reconciliation.

Jesus of Nazareth taught the principle of inclusion by his radical elevation of unconditional love as a sociopolitical principle. Jesus repudiated barriers of gender, tribe, religion, class and caste, and ideology in establishing a social practice of inclusivity. In the New Testament, the basis for this practice of inclusivity is unconditional love or agape. Therein love is described not merely as friendship or affection within families. It is not merely passion or love between sexes. Rather, it is compassionate self-giving and sacrifice on behalf of "the other" that originates as a volitional act, a deliberate choice of the heart. Jesus clearly understood the application of unconditional love or embrace to both relationships between individuals and between communities. Buddha described it as loving kindness (*metta*) and compassion (karuna). Mahatma Gandhi actually sought to give it political shape in his mission of nonviolent reconciliation in the Asian subcontinent.

So who is worthy of such unconditional love from us? Our spouse or children? Our parents or siblings? Our friends and supporters? Who is worthy of such unconditional love from our community or nation? Our sister cities or trading partners? Our allies and those who support our policies and national interests? Jesus answered that complex dilemma by revisiting a simple rhetorical question from the Torah provoked by the conflict between Cain and Abel. "Who is my neighbor?" is a question that should echo not only in the souls of individuals but also in the souls of communities and nations. It hints at the seemingly absurd notion of love as a political principle.

Rarely do we think of love as a political principle. To many in the realm of political, economic, diplomatic, or national security structures, the concept of unconditional love as an organizing principle seems, at best, naïve and, at worst, dangerous and incomprehensible. It is dismissed with a polite chuckle and an admonition that love has no place in the policy maker's calculus especially in the realm of realpolitik, which is defined by power and national interest. Can we seriously suggest that in a world of interest-group politics and economic self-determination that unconditional love should be embraced by the polis, by the citizens of a community? Can we seriously suggest that in a world of militants and rogue states that unconditional love is a principle that should define national interest and the relationships between sovereign states? The Abrahamic tradition would say yes. Jesus of Nazareth would say yes. Muhammed would say yes. Gautama Buddha would say yes. Guru Nanak Dev would say yes. Mahatma Gandhi and Martin Luther King Jr. would say yes. Each of these visionary figures were guided by a worldview that assumed an integrated approach to the religious and political realms. The realist would dismiss such visionary figures as idealists who are so heavenly minded as to be no earthly good. In contrast, the realist is guided by a worldview that would assume a segregation of faith and politics, in which religion is viewed both as something for the private sphere and as a primary cause of conflict in the world. This latter worldview in actuality provides no basis for hope and leads to a humanistic cynicism grounded in fear. In the post-September 11 domestic and international order, the realistic worldview demands an overwhelming obsession with security, which is derived from fear of "the other," to whom we owe nothing but implacable hostility. At the core of both worldviews is the difficult question of how we respond to walls of hostility both in ourselves and in the other.

The principle of inclusion as one of the core values of faith-based reconciliation requires us as individuals and as identity-based groups to come face-to-face with the walls of hostility that lurk in our own heart toward groups that differ from us or hate us or even attack us. Walls are an essential ingredient in the daily life of almost every culture. Walls play a positive role in holding up a dwelling or structure, establishing boundaries or a property line, or enabling confinement of small children. Walls can provide protection, refuge, or privacy. However, walls of hostility are those that are erected between individuals, communities, or nations that are built on foundations of isolation, ignorance, fear, prejudice, or hatred. Walls of hostility might be evidenced by mental or behavior traits, bad feeling, opposition, antagonism, or even conflict or warfare. Walls of hostility might be constructed from beliefs, class distinctions, history, folklore, prejudices, tastes, and values. However, the sacred texts reveal that hostility is more than an attitude; it is a part of our fundamental human condition—that part of us that is separated from God and others. Some years ago, I was participating in a study group at my church about the subject of healing historical wounds. One woman in the group suggested that the United States should apologize to Japan for the bombings at Hiroshima and Nagasaki in August 1945. Being a postwar baby boomer, I felt myself stiffen and began to bristle. I thought to myself, *There is no way we should apologize to the Japanese for an action that was necessary to break the back of their militaristic spirit.* As I reflected in silence on my thoughts, I realized that a wall of hostility in my own heart had been exposed to me.

Facing up to our own hostility may be one of the most difficult, painful, and courageous things that we can do. It is particularly difficult for people of faith or altruistic people who see themselves as loving everyone and harboring hostility toward no one. Nevertheless, coming face-to-face with our own hostility is absolutely essential to the dynamic of reconciliation. It is the first step in the sociopolitical healing process. Often, when one becomes a proactive agent of reconciliation, one finds oneself working with the very group who was the target of hostility. It is an especially important function for leaders to empower their own constituencies to dismantle or scale the walls of hostility. Communities will generally mimic the hostility of their leaders, but they will also eventually follow their lead in reaching out to embrace "the other."

Both the sacred texts and human experience would point to three fundamental walls of hostility: gender, class, and tribe. First, let us consider the dimensions of gender hostility. The manifestation of gender hostility may be as seemingly benign or innocuous as a failure to understand each other (i.e., women are from Venus; men are from Mars) or the gender bashing that occurs in single-sex gatherings. On the other hand, it may be as malignant as spousal battering, rape, economic injustice, or male domination of the instruments of power in a society. The first chapter of the Book of Genesis teaches us that both men and women are created in the image or attributes of God. As such, both are the crown or apex of God's creation and are worthy of respect and dignity. From the very beginning, God puts the stamp of approval on gender diversity. However, the third chapter of the Book of Genesis teaches us that both male and female used their own free will to transgress the boundaries of God's sovereignty. One of the primary consequences of that choice was the beginning of gender alienation, where sexual differences became a source of profound estrangement rather than affirmation, mutuality, and interdependence. We are living today with the results of that choice. In many religious traditions, there is an insistence, often buttressed from certain verses from the sacred text on male leadership of the community. I have often found myself wondering if the insistence on male leadership is an expression of God's perfect will for human social organization or an unfortunate reflection of its broken, fallen nature.

Second, let us consider the dimensions of class hostility. The manifestations of class hostility may be as seemingly benign or normal as between the blue bloods of British upper class and their servants in an English countryside estate. On the other hand, it may be as malignant as repressive oligarchic rule by a privileged elite or popular revolution by the people leading to anarchy and terrorism. In a sense, Marxism as a form of historical materialism grew out of profound class alienation. In the same sense, one of the driving forces behind the worldwide network of terrorism is a profound sense of alienation with an international system run by and for the benefit of Western elites in cooperation with their proxies in Africa, Asia, Latin America, and the Middle East. However, behind the rise of Marxism and international terrorism is a much more disturbing question. Why do class differences exist? Are class differences created by God or by human sin?

Class or caste seems endemic to almost every culture. Such factors as hereditary titles, family prominence, economic wealth, education, profession or occupation, manners, and breeding all play a complex role in defining class identity. However, at a deeper level, we all have a sense of "our kind of people": European intellectuals and the working class, Indian Brahmins and Dalits, Mexican landowners and peasants, and Rwandan Tutsis and Hutus are all aware that they are different from each other and that, clearly, there is a sense of social stratification. In 1991, as my wife and I stood on the front porch of former East German president Erich Honecker in Wandlitz, an upscale walled-in community outside of East Berlin, we realized how much the preaching of the communists about creating the perfect classless society was a sham. Communism in East Germany had simply created a new oligarchy centered around Communist party membership.

Jesus of Nazareth, in his preaching about the kingdom or reign of God, and Guru Nanak Dev, the founder of Sikhism, envisioned a society wherein class barriers were transcended by the politics of love as an inherent feature of a moral vision of faith-based reconciliation. Jesus intentionally began his mission among the despised classes of Galilee instead of the privileged elite of Jerusalem. The Sikh concept of the *langar* or community kitchen was meant to overcome the strong caste prejudices of the Indian subcontinent. Muhammed taught his followers that there was no divine basis for class superiority (Surah 49:13). In essence, class and caste is a human creation that engenders hostility or estrangement between groups of people based on social location and values. It fulfills our fallen human need to feel superior to "the other." It also permits the privileged and wealthy to regard their advantages as matters of right rather than considering the moral implications of privilege.

Third, let us consider the dimensions of tribal hostility. The world is seeing a resurgence of tribalism, which offers common identity to the alienated, roots to the rootless, security to the fearful, power to the powerless, significance to the small in stature, and belonging to the forlorn. Tribalism includes four principle manifestations: racism, nationalism, anti-Semitism, and ethnoreligious communalism.

Racism might be defined as prejudice coupled with power. It takes a number of different forms such as genocide, deportation, apartheid, structural racism, and assimilationist racism. Professor Harlan L. Dalton in his book, *Racial Healing*, states that racism has everything to do with the distribution of power and privilege in a society. One racial group has advantage over another simply because of its race. He points out that we must be honest with ourselves to admit that race matters and that it confers advantages on one group and disadvantages on another group. He also states that the powerful group tends to take its race for granted. By contrast, the powerless groups are very aware of their race—blacks in America, gypsies in east Central Europe, black Africans in Sudan. In essence, racism centers on race-based animosity, disliking someone for their race and acting in ways that create and reproduce racial hierarchy by defending social advantages for the privileged group. I am convinced that racial healing between Anglos and African Americans in the United States is fundamental to addressing one of our deepest wounds and releasing the fullness of our potential as a nation. For both groups, this will be painful. For Anglos, it will mean having to wrestle with how they continue to benefit from a system of white privilege and how that can be changed. For African Americans, it will mean giving up suffering as a badge of honor and discovering a new identity within American society.

Nationalism involves placing the nation or people group on a sacred pedestal as the object of one's highest loyalty. The nation is consecrated and becomes a holy entity. Service—even death for the sake of the nation's survival—cohesion, and glory are elevated to the level of sacrifice and martyrdom. In nationalism, the religious is secularized and the national sanctified. One must make a distinction between nationalism and patriotism. Patriotism as love and loyalty to one's homeland is healthy and admirable. However, nationalism involves attitudes and behaviors that view one's own ethnic group or culture as inherently superior to others. It can lead to the arrogant assumption that one's culture or ethnic group is justified in exploiting, dominating, or imposing its way of life on others. Many conservative evangelical Christians operate with the assumption that what is good for America is good for God. Many Jewish and Christian Zionists blindly support any policy of the Israeli government regardless of whether or not it is just in its treatment of Palestinians. Many Muslim militants and even moderates support any policy that "pokes America in the eyes" or undermines the Israelis.

One might broaden the meaning of nation to include three distinct types of people groups: political entities such as nation-states; ethnic groupings such as Kurds, Kashmiris, or Latinos; and religious communities such as Jews, Christians, Muslims, Hindus, Buddhists, and Sikhs. With respect to political entities, we can point to long-standing hostility between the United States and Cuba, between India and Pakistan, Greece and Turkey, and Israel and Syria. With respect to ethnic groupings, we can point to long-standing hostility between Koreans and Japanese, Kurds and Turks, Serbs and Bosnian Muslims, and Anglos and Latinos in America. With respect to religious communities, we can point to long-standing hostility between Hindus and Muslims in Gujarat, Catholics and Protestants in Northern Ireland, Christians and Muslims in Sudan, and Buddhists and Hindus in Sri Lanka. Even within confessional communities, one discovers intense hostility such as Evangelicals and Catholics in Latin America, Russian Orthodox and Pentecostals in Russia, Sunnis and Shias in Iraq, and Reformed and Orthodox Jews in Israel. Within the religious communities, I would like to dwell for a moment on the hostility within the Abrahamic tradition among Jews, Christians, and Muslims. Three great religious traditions, over three billion people on the face of the earth, trace their spiritual roots and identity back to the patriarch who heard the divine voice beckoning him to a promised land and made that first step from Ur and Haran to Hebron. Historically, each community has used its Abrahamic identity as a means of establishing its uniqueness and superiority. Jews began describing themselves as the true children of Abraham in the wake of returning from exile in Babylon in the fifth century BCE. Christians began describing themselves as the true children of Abraham in the first century CE experience of persecution by both the mainline Jewish community and the Roman authorities. Muslims began describing themselves as the true children of Abraham in the seventh century as Muhammed's message was largely rejected by the Jewish and Christian communities. Jews trace their lineage to Abraham through Isaac and Moses. Christians trace their roots to Abraham through Isaac and Jesus. Muslims trace their genealogical roots through Ishmael and Esau. Two sons, Ishmael and Isaac, were pitted against each other by a father's favoritism and a mother's jealousy. Isaac became the child of promise. Ishmael, the elder child, experienced rejection, not at the hands of God but at the hands of a human father. We live with the consequences of that spiritual and emotional wound to this day. Jews, Christians, and Muslims have had a long history of hostility toward one another. A family, yes! But a dysfunctional family at best. Today, the vast majority of interstate and intrastate conflicts involve one or more parts of the Abrahamic family. Clearly, there will be no peace in the twenty-first century until there is healing in the broken family of Abraham. Bruce Feiler in his book, *Abraham: A Journey to the Heart of Three Faiths,* raises the possibility of rediscovering Abraham as a universalizing figure, as a faith-based *über reconciler* for the twenty-first century. Perhaps we need to heed the words of the prophet Isaiah (Is 51:1-2) by returning to our roots, by returning to the core of the Abrahamic tradition and mission, and by rediscovering Abraham.

Let us turn our attention to the most difficult dimension of healing the broken family of Abraham—anti-Semitism. Anti-Semitism has come to mean hostility toward the Jewish people and, more recently, the state of Israel, in spite of the fact that Arabs are also Semitic people. Hostility toward the Jewish people represents the longest sustained form of hatred against any people group in human history. It can be traced back some thirty centuries and includes such decisive events as slavery under pharaoh in Egypt, ethnic cleansing by Haman in Persia, the destruction of Israel and Jerusalem by the Romans, the Christian Crusades of the Middle Ages, and the European Holocaust under the Nazis, which led to the death of six million Jews. Anti-Semitism is both a historical reality and a present danger, particularly in its resurgence in post-Christian Europe and its growth in the Islamic world. I have come to a deep appreciation of the unique nature of the Shoah or the Holocaust through my friendship with two Jewish

Holocaust survivors, Ruth Nebel and Nina Morecki, as well as pilgrimages to Auschwitz, Dachau, Sachsenhausen, Ravensbruck, and Terezenstadt. It has sensitized me to the subtle signs of anti-Semitism that can take root in the hearts of individuals and communities. In my community of Santa Barbara, there have been at least two public incidents of anti-Semitism in the form of swastikas painted on the windows of Jewish-owned businesses.

Ethnoreligious communalism involves the construction of religion as a political collective, bringing together four key ingredients: politics, religious identity, militancy, and occult spiritual power. Religion can serve as a powerful social cement that binds together racial, linguistic, class, and territorial elements of identity. At the same time, when religion and politics are integrated with militancy, they become an explosive mixture fueled by hatred. At the heart of any militant movement is not the cause but the most extreme forms of hostility in the hatred of "the other." In their heart of hearts, militants are motivated to destroy "the other." They perceive "the other" as their sworn enemies. The common spiritual, social, and psychological thread of militant groups—whether Al-Qaeda, Hamas, Hezbollah, Aryan Nations, Neo-Nazis, or the Ku Klux Klan is hatred grounded in a deep sense of woundedness. The answer to fighting terrorism is not simply removing the gun from the hand of the militant or terminating him with extreme prejudice. One must deal with the ideas behind the gun that motivates him to pick up the gun in the first place.

So how do we demolish walls of hostility? Let us consider four aspects of the reconciler's task. First is the transformation of the human heart, transformation of hostility into love. What is it that causes people or communities to embrace hostility toward each other? Is it possible for hostility in the human heart to be transformed? Dr. Martin Luther King Jr., who was the target of so much hate during the course of the African-American Civil Rights Movement, offered a key insight in his book *Strength to Love*. King posited that hostility or hate is more than an emotion; it is a spiritual force of demonic origin that can take over the entire soul—distorting the personality, destroying a person's sense of values and objectivity and setting them on a destructive path. As King observed in Southern segregationists and as I have observed in Kashmiri militants, we become vulnerable to hostility and hate through experiences of woundedness caused by painful experiences in our life. King observed from his experience that it was only the supernatural power of God that could transform a person's heart. I have observed this same truth at work in the world's roughest neighborhood, Kashmir. In our seminars on faith-based reconciliation, we have brought together estranged communities such as Kashmiri Muslims and pandits. The seminar would begin in a climate of intense hostility, yet, over the course of four days, the two communities discovered "the other" at a new and deeper level, which enabled God to change their hearts and effect a dynamic of reconciliation. This work of transformation is one that faith-based reconcilers understand and can engender much more deeply than their secular counterparts can.

Second is the love for one's enemies. An enemy is one with whom we have an antagonistic relationship, and there exists some measure of hostility. An enemy may wish us harm, may seek to damage our interests or reputation with other parties. They might interpret all our words and actions by assuming the worst motives or evil intentions behind them. One of the unique aspects of Jesus's teaching is the principle of love for one's enemies. It represents one of the most radical but also one of the most powerful aspects of his teaching when it is applied into situations of intense conflict. In the work of faith-based reconciliation in the Episcopal Church, I have personally experienced the dynamic of loving and being loved by my enemies. Several of our team members who were on the other side of the conflict from me acknowledged that they once viewed me as an enemy, but God changed their hearts, and, through that divine action, we became friends.

Loving one's enemy begins in a climate of truth telling by acknowledging the evil words or actions that the enemy has committed toward you, but it recognizes that it does not express all that he or she is. As Martin Luther King Jr. observed, an element of goodness may be found even in our worst enemy. However, the heart of loving our enemy is discovered in the experience of forgiveness even as we continue the pursuit of justice. Forgiveness and justice held in tension is the heart of loving our enemy. The pursuit of justice without forgiveness becomes, in reality, revenge motivated by hatred. It is the act of forgiveness that distinguishes between justice and revenge.

Third is the exorcising of demons. Walls of hostility can cause us to demonize our enemy. To demonize another person means that we see all their characteristics, hear all their words, and view all their actions from a negative or adversarial perspective. It means that we assume the worst motives and evil intentions behind their words and actions. It means we present them in a negative or adversarial manner to third parties in order to damage their reputation or interests. We easily personalize our differences of ethnicity, culture, religion, or ideology. To exorcise those demons, we must confess and acknowledge our own hard-heartedness. We must acknowledge our inability to love the person or group we have demonized, ask God to change our heart, and develop specific changed behaviors toward the enemy. In the conflict over human sexuality in the Episcopal Church, one of my friends and fellow reconcilers confessed that she could remember at one time thinking of me as "the Antichrist."

Another friend and fellow reconciler once described me to friends as the "Darth Vader of the Episcopal Church".

Fourth is the practice of ethical speech. Rabbi Joseph Telushkin in his book, *Words That Hurt, Words That Heal: How to Use Words Wisely and Well*, points out that the Jewish tradition views words both as tangible and extremely powerful. Both the sacred texts and historical experience teach the potency of the spoken word. Words are double-edged. Without words, poetry would not exist, but neither could war. Words can be used to hurt or to bring healing to others. Words that hurt include criticism, excessive anger, sarcasm, public and private humiliation, hurtful nicknames, betrayal of secrets, rumors, lies, malicious gossip, slander, and threats. Words that heal include expressions of caring, concern, gratitude, and affirmation. So, in demolishing the walls of hostility, we must be prepared to examine our own pattern of spoken words and embrace the practice of ethical speech. In the midst of intense conflict, it is not unusual to refer to members of the other side in pejorative terms. This is particularly a common practice on American talk show programs, which rarely assume good or sincere intentions by people on the other side.

In conclusion, compassionate inclusion is the second core value of faith-based reconciliation, and the means to its implementation is demolishing walls of hostility.

Chapter Five

CONFLICT RESOLUTION
THE PRINCIPLE OF PEACEMAKING

Peacemaking means that we seek the peaceful resolution of conflicts between individuals and groups.

In 2002, I was part of a meeting at the U.S. State Department with officials concerned with South Asia and with international religious freedom. My colleague, Dr. Douglas Johnston, and I shared with them about the work of the Washington DC-based International Center for Religion and Diplomacy and explained our methodology of faith-based diplomacy. We also described our project of faith-based reconciliation in Kashmir and our hopes for creating a transformational environment and a cooperative spirit on both sides of the Line of Control between India and Pakistan as a prelude to a series of bridge building meetings. When we concluded our presentation, one official remarked, "Nothing else has worked in Kashmir; we might as well give faith a chance."

Two years earlier in September 2000, my colleague, Professor Daniel Philpott, and I traveled to Delhi as faith-based diplomats armed only with our trust in God's providence and a list of names and telephone numbers provided to me by former national security advisor Bud Mc Farlane and the late Dr. Haneef Ramay, a senior Pakistani political leader. The first person who agreed to see us was Professor Kamal Chenoy, a professor of international relations at Jawaharlal Nehru University, an avowed Marxist and a passionate human rights activist. Considering that we were people of faith, we were surprised and elated that he was willing to assist our venture. Nevertheless, he could not have been more gracious and helpful. As we sipped tea in his living room on the university campus, he briefed us on key Kashmiri personalities and facts about the conflict. Later in that journey, we met with many key Kashmiri leaders in Srinagar and Jammu and with Indian leaders in Delhi. It was only then that we began to truly appreciate the complex and sobering realities that made Kashmir one of the world's roughest neighborhoods and an intractable identity-based conflict.

I am a trained professional mediator. As such, I have been well trained in the tools of conflict analysis, negotiation, and mediation that enables a third-party intermediary to assist the conflicting parties in crafting a negotiated settlement. However, as I became involved in the conflict in Kashmir, it became clear to me over time that the traditional tools of diplomacy and conflict resolution were inadequate to approach an intractable identity-based conflict, particularly one in which religion was a key ingredient in communal identity.

Conflict seems inherently woven into the tapestry of life. The Jewish scriptures describe the first conflict between husband and wife in the Garden of Eden over who was responsible for transgressing the boundaries of God's sovereignty. The second recorded conflict took place between two brothers, Cain and Abel. It ended with violence and death for one and banishment for the other. All human beings at one time or another become embroiled in conflict situations—whether in marriage, family, business, or social spheres. Conflicts range in scope from domestic spats to wars between nations. Sometimes a conflict is merely a war of words, and, at other times, the conflict might involve lethal weapons or even sophisticated high technology armaments.

Peacemaking is a noble human venture that seeks to resolve conflict by peaceful means. It assumes that conflict is not only a part of the tapestry of life but that it can be a healthy expression of wrestling with differences. Sometimes conflicts can and should be avoided. However, when that is no longer possible or when the perceived costs of avoidance exceed the costs of confrontation, the skilled heart and hands of a peacemaker can guide the conflicting parties to the negotiating table to talk about the conflict in a respectful manner and engage in joint problem solving to resolve the issues and restore the relationships.

Within the Christian community, the Mennonites and Quakers have traditionally been known as peace churches. Historically, the role of peacemaking has not played a significant role in the mission of Catholic, Anglican, or Evangelical churches. I am not aware of traditions within Judaism or Islam that have sought to emphasize peacemaking as a primary religious mission. However, given the nature of the twenty-first century and the volume of conflicts, I am personally committed to raising up an army of reconcilers from the various religious traditions. When I first traveled to Sarajevo in Bosnia in 1996, I discovered that the Jewish community was perfectly positioned to play a peacemaking/reconciling role among Catholics, Orthodox, and Muslims. The Jewish community was small and, hence, a threat to no one, and it had not been involved in the conflict. Dr. Jacob Vinci, president of the Jewish community, agreed with me. Together, we undertook to bring the grand mufti, Dr. Ceric, together with Cardinal Puljic from the Croat Catholic community and Metropolitan Irenej from the Serbian Orthodox community. However, a bombing of several Muslim homes in Brcko by Serb paramilitaries made it impossible for the grand mufti, despite his heart for reconciliation, to come together at that time. Later, through the skilled efforts of Dr. Landrum Bolling, who worked under the auspices of several agencies, these leaders were brought together in Vienna.

Faith-based peacemakers seek to integrate the tools of conflict resolution with the texts, traditions, and practices of their religious tradition. Prayer, fasting, spiritual conversations, reading from the sacred texts, apologies, and forgiveness will play as vital a role as negotiation, exploration of settlement frameworks, generating options, and making concessions. Faith-based peacemakers also place a high value on restoration of personal relationships. A negotiated settlement that leaves the parties mired in anger, resentment, and unforgiveness is not acceptable to the faith-based peacemaker. The goal of a faith-based intervention is not only a sustainable negotiated settlement but also a transformation of the relationships and the hearts of the parties toward each other.

Jesus of Nazareth taught and modeled the principle of peacemaking. In the Sermon on the Mount, one of Mahatma Gandhi's favorite portions of sacred text, Jesus said, "Blessed are the peacemakers for they shall be called children of God." (Matthew 5:9) Jesus taught his followers that to avoid conflict in certain situations by "turning the other cheek" was an appropriate moral choice. He also taught his followers a four-step dispute resolution process involving negotiation, mediation, and arbitration. (Matthew 18:15-20)

In the Jewish tradition, the Book of Exodus tells us how Moses was directed by God to choose arbitrators for the community of Israel to settle disputes. Historically, an important rabbinic function has been to serve as an arbitrator of disputes within the Jewish community. In the Qu'ran, believers are exhorted to make peace between conflicting parties as a means of demonstrating fear of God. At times, Muhammed served as a mediator in disputes involving the emerging Islamic community and the Jews of

Yathrib (Medina). Mahatma Gandhi incarnated the Hindu approach to conflict resolution in his strategy of nonviolent noncooperation against the British colonial occupation. In the Buddhist tradition, the dharma is meant to create an ethic of nonviolent peace activism and conflict resolution. Sikhism arose as an attempt to find a peaceful resolution to the Hindu and Muslim conflict in the Indian subcontinent.

At this point, it seems appropriate to provide definitions of conflict and dispute. The first definition is derived from basic conflict resolution textbooks:

> A conflict exists when two parties have perceived divergence of interests which are translated into rigid, incompatible aspirations and where there are no available alternatives to fulfill those aspirations and there exists a climate of intense distrust.

However, based on my experience of international faith-based conflict resolution in such places as Bosnia, Kosovo, Burundi, Kashmir, and Sudan, I have found that the classical definition is often inadequate to capture the spiritual and sociopolitical complexities of many conflicts. Hence, I would like to describe an additional type of conflict:

> A conflict exists when there has been a violation of the moral grain of the universe in a society or between nations such as a lack of respect for diversity, a historic or existing injustice, a violation of God's sovereignty by one people group seeking to dominate another, or an unhealed people group becoming captive to a bitter history and deciding to settle old scores.

Finally, there is the basic conflict resolution textbook definition of a dispute:

> A dispute begins as a grievance: an individual's belief that he/she is entitled to a resource that someone else may grant or deny. People respond to a grievance in one of three ways: lump it, redefine the problem and redirect the blame, or register the blame or register a claim, which communicates a sense of entitlement to the party perceived to be responsible. If the claim is rejected as a whole or in part then a dispute exists between the two parties.

Christopher W. Moore in his book, *The Mediation Process*, describes five different types of conflicts. *Relationship* conflicts are caused by strong emotions, poor communication, misperceptions, stereotypes, or repetitive

50

negative behavior. *Data* conflicts are caused by lack of information, misinformation, different viewpoints, different interpretations, or different assessment procedures. *Interest* conflicts are caused by perceived or actual competition over claiming value in a zero-sum exchange. *Structural* conflicts are caused by destructive patterns of behavior, unequal distribution of resources, unequal power, or time constraints. *Value* conflicts are caused by different core criteria for evaluating ideas or behavior, different ways of life, ideology, or religion.

The works of Jay Rothman and Louise Diamond point to a sixth type of conflict known as identity-based conflict. This type of conflict, which is the primary focus of faith-based reconciliation, is rooted in a people group's collective identity and their need for self-determination, security, community, and vitality. Identity-based conflicts might also arise out of collective fears, interests, or need of honor. I began chapter 2 by stating that in many respects both national and international politics of the twenty-first century have become the politics of identity. This implies that cross-cultural differences serve as a primary factor in conflict. I have discovered through my experiences in Africa, Asia, Europe, and the Middle East that religion often plays a critical role in identity-based conflict. In Kashmir, whether one is Muslim or Hindu is a key factor in collective identity. In Sudan, whether one is Muslim or Christian defines "us vs. them." In Northern Ireland, whether one is Catholic or Protestant defines the contours of the conflict. Religion may not be the principal cause of the conflict, but it provides a key part of collective identity. Thus, to ignore faith and religion in conflict analysis or modes of intervention is to not only miss a critical dimension; it is to foolishly omit potentially rich assets for peacemaking.

Faith-based reconciliation has a distinctive approach to conflict analysis and modes of intervention. Yet it has the capacity to work constructively with other forms of track-two diplomacy and official initiatives of track-one diplomacy. Track-one diplomacy comprises official government-to-government interaction whereas track-two diplomacy describes a host of initiatives by nonstate actors from the religious, business, professional, or humanitarian sectors. Hence, this potential for organic linkage between track-one and track-two diplomacy is an important consideration for policy makers and diplomats, particularly in situations where religion is a key part of the conflict. Faith-based reconcilers can provide crucial insights into the religious dimension of conflicts such as motivations and methodologies of faith-based actors, which might be misunderstood by the secular intermediary. Studying comparative religion and being factually knowledgeable about the history and theology of a particular faith tradition is not the same thing as submitting one's will, intellect, and emotions to the authority of God. Acknowledging and submitting to a transcendent authority influences one's worldview, analysis, and modes of intervention. In ICRD's work in Kashmir over the past five years, we have regularly met with senior level officials in Delhi and Islamabad and also with members of the diplomatic community in an effort to create this organic linkage between track-one and track-two diplomacy as well as bringing faith-based perspectives for their consideration.

An analysis of any conflict begins by asking standard, basic questions: Who are the parties? What is this conflict about? What are the main issues and the stated positions of the parties on the issues? What are the underlying needs, values, interests, and fears of the parties? What was the cause of the conflict? What strategic choices have the parties made to resolve the conflict? What is the stage of the conflict, and how has it evolved over time? What is the desired outcome of the conflict, and how do the parties define their aspirations? Is a negotiated settlement possible? Is there a potential zone of agreement? What are the bottom lines and BATNAs (best alternative to a negotiated agreement) of the parties? What role do third parties play? What are the benefits and costs to the parties of continuing the conflict? What is the relative power differential and resources of the parties? What factors contribute to stability? What previous initiatives for peacemaking have been undertaken, and what were the results? As an agency engaged in faith-based diplomacy, ICRD officials begin the process of intervention by meeting people at all levels of the society and listening carefully to them. We ask the same questions over and over again in an effort to develop an on-the-ground perspective of the conflict.

However, faith-based analysis recognizes the limits of human wisdom including the discipline of conflict analysis and relies on the teaching of the sacred texts to ascertain a transcendent dimension on the nature of the human heart and behavior. First of all, the sacred texts teach us that the primary root of conflict and war is human sin, which tells us that conflict is a moral problem that reveals something about the condition of the human heart. This leads us to ask the following questions: what is the spiritual orientation of the parties? To what extent is pride, hardness of heart, or self-interest driving the conflict? Do the parties possess the humility to look into their own hearts, which might lead to repentance and a change of behavior? What sort of circumstances might prompt and facilitate such reflection? To what extent are the parties concerned for themselves, and to what extent are they concerned for each other? In ICRD's work of reconciliation with Kashmiri Muslims and pandits, we discovered by listening to their hearts that underneath all the anger and hostility was a deep yearning to be together again and restore *Kashmiriyat*.

The sacred texts also teach us that conflict is an inevitable result when individuals or groups take sovereignty into their own hands, following their own autonomous wills and purposes. People in a conflict frequently allow feelings and motivations such as revenge, anger, temptation, or ambition to take control of their lives. For reconciliation to occur, they must submit or resubmit to a new authority in their lives, the authority of God. This leads a faith-based reconciler to ask the following questions: to what extent have the parties made an act of submission to God? Can they remember an experience of surrendering their will to God? To what extent does God's will and purposes even matter to them? In what ways do they view their conflict behavior as consistent with submission to God? To what extent are the leaders of a community open to spiritual and moral principles as a basis for governance and accountability? In what ways does religion play a role in the conflict? In what ways have religious leaders been part of the problem or part of the solution? In what way have religious teachings fostered the conflict? In a July 2002 faith-based reconciliation seminar bringing Kashmiri Muslims and pandits together for the first time in ICRD's work, I said to the Muslim members of the team, "Today, we will find out if you are true Muslims." They looked puzzled and inquired about the meaning of my words. I explained, "By definition, a Muslim is a person who is submitted to God. One aspect of being submitted to God is having a humble heart. Today, you will hear some very painful things said by pandits about Muslims. You will be tempted to respond to set the record straight. You will be tempted to justify yourselves and strike back. Resist those temptations. Today, you must be willing to listen and respond to the pain and suffering of your pandit brothers and sisters."

The sacred texts also teach us that conflict is an inevitable result when societies and states violate the moral grain of the universe with respect to pluralism and social justice. In many societies today, an intolerance for diversity or an unwillingness to share privilege are the deep-seated roots of long-term systemic conflict. The desire by one group to dominate another, violations of human rights, religious persecution, or inequitable distribution of privilege each preclude true and full reconciliation. This leads us to ask the following questions: what are the core values of the parties? Where do their core values overlap, and where do they clash? Has there been an historic injustice that needs to be acknowledged and remedied? Is there a present situation of injustice that makes settlement difficult or impossible? Are one or both of the parties engaged in evil activity such as genocide or ethnic cleansing for which there can be no compromise? Is there freedom of religion? What is the tolerance level for diversity in the parties? Regardless of the many legitimate perspectives on the conflict in Kashmir, there is one simple truth: until the British and Indian governments are prepared to acknowledge and remedy the historic injustices in Kashmir, there will be no true reconciliation.

Finally, the sacred texts teach us that conflict is an inevitable result when there are unhealed wounds in the collective memory of a community. Parties that are captive to a bitter history will find it extremely difficult to live in peace with each other. In many cases, it only takes a manipulative political, religious, or social movement leader to reawaken painful memories that stir groups to violence and conflict as we have witnessed in such places as the Balkans, Burundi, Rwanda, or Kashmir. This fact prompts the following questions: what historical wounds remain unhealed which make settlement difficult or impossible? How do the parties understand and interpret their history? What internal and external factors have caused or contributed to the historical wounds? Will the conflict between Israelis and Palestinians remain unsolved as long as it is approached in a traditional conflict resolution mode? Will there ever be true peace until one addresses the historical wounds of an ancient family feud in the family of Abraham?

Now let us consider modes of conflict intervention. A faith-based actor values the tools of negotiation and mediation in assisting parties to come to a settlement of the conflict. In negotiation, the parties speak directly with each other about their differences and seek to craft a mutually satisfactory settlement of the conflict. There are three basic methods of negotiation: cooperative bargaining, distributive bargaining, and integrative bargaining. The method that is closest to the ethic of the sacred texts is integrative bargaining, which is also known as principled negotiation or the problem-solving approach. Roger Fisher and William Ury in their book, *Getting to YES*, describe principled negotiation as a process of coming to a solution without destroying a relationship. Principled negotiation embodies five key principles. First of all, expand the pie so as to create value for the parties, and, thus, the negotiation becomes a nonzero-sum activity, where one party's gain is not the other party's loss. Second, be soft on people even if you are resolute on the issues. The parties should negotiate in a climate of mutual respect. Third, go "below the line" to focus on the deeper interests, needs, and fears of the parties rather than the stated positions. This will engender a higher level of creativity. Fourth, generate options that will lead to a mutually satisfactory settlement. Fifth, utilize objective criteria for evaluating options rather than subjective self-interest.

Principled negotiation is an approach, in which the faith-based actor seeks to reframe the conflict in three ways: first, as a common problem to be solved by the parties in which they need each other for its resolution; second, as an ethical challenge to seek a resolution that is just for all the parties; third, as an opportunity for transformation of the hearts of the parties. It might be said that these three characteristics are not unique to faith-based actors but rather govern the approach of any principled negotiator. Hence, while they are not unique to faith-based conflict intervention, they are essential to define its character.

Mediation is an informal but structured process in which one or more third parties assist the disputants to talk about the conflict and negotiate a solution. The process is designed to empower the parties to construct their own settlement, not impose a binding solution on the parties. The mediation process seeks to accomplish six basic tasks. First, it seeks to bring the parties to the negotiation table. Second, it seeks to create a climate of trust, cooperation, and constructive communication. Third, it enables the parties to present their perceptions of the conflict including their needs, hopes, fears, and values. Fourth, it enables the parties to discuss settlement frameworks that set the stage for generating detailed options and negotiating a solution. Fifth, it enables the parties to explore creative options and negotiate over them. Sixth, it memorializes the agreement with accountability, enforcement, and confidence-building measures. In the conflict resolution process, the parties must be willing to look both at themselves and at each other. In searching one's own heart, a party must ask, "What are my needs? What do I value? What do I fear? What are my highest aspirations? What is my bottom line? How do I feel about this conflict and about the other party?" In looking into the face of the person across the mediation table, a party must be willing to hear the other party, because people will not engage in problem solving until they have felt heard.

In an identity-based conflict, particularly one involving long-term estrangement and violence, a faith-based actor seeks to reframe the conflict by constructing a faith-based reconciliation framework as the methodology of intervention. A faith-based reconciliation framework represents a different lens than a strict conflict resolution approach because it considers the spiritual and moral dimensions of intervention as well as the political, social, economic, and psychological factors. John Paul Lederach, in drawing from Psalm 85:10 of the Jewish scriptures, captures the heart of this approach in identifying four key elements of the healing process: truth, mercy, justice, and peace. Truth values transparency, honesty, and clarity. Mercy values people, relationships, compassion, and the frailty of the human condition. Justice values accountability, what is right, fairness, equity and remedies for oppression, exploitation, or tyranny. Peace values security, respect, and well-being. As Lederach writes in his book, *The Journey Toward Reconciliation*, "The meeting place of these four elements in union is reconciliation."

A faith-based reconciliation framework applied to an identity-based conflict seeks to bring about a resolution of the conflict, restoration of the political order that has suffered war and injustice, and the reconciliation of people groups. As such, it consists of six basic elements: imparting moral vision, building bridges between estranged groups, a peace accord, advocacy for social justice, political forgiveness, and healing deep collective wounds.

Societies engulfed in or emerging from violent conflict need a fresh moral vision on which to build or rebuild political, economic, social, and cultural structures. Faith-based reconciliation is just such a moral vision that provides the strategic basis for hope and healing. A faith-based actor in conflict situations seeks to impart the moral vision of faith-based reconciliation to senior, civil society, and grassroots leaders. In the case of senior level leaders such as heads of state, government ministers, members of parliament, cardinals, chief rabbis, grand muftis, or national social movement leaders, impartation of moral vision is best accomplished through personal meetings. On the civil society or grassroots level, the methodology of a seminar or civil society forums can be vehicles for disseminating the core values of faith-based reconciliation. During the years that I was involved in the work of faith-based reconciliation in east Central Europe, I had private meetings with several heads of state. In those meetings, I would always seek to impress upon them their unique role in the nation and the opportunity to articulate a moral vision of faith-based reconciliation. In the case of one head of state, I later learned that after our initial meeting that the word "reconciliation" began to appear regularly in his speeches on television and in his meetings with the national leadership of various ethnic groups. In our many meetings with Kashmiri separatist leaders over the years, we would always bring up the subject of reconciliation. After approximately three years, we discovered that their press releases and public speeches began to include calls for reconciliation.

Conflict, particularly violent protracted conflict, destroys the social fabric of society or region and, hence, requires the faith-based actor to build bridges between estranged groups of people. In Kashmir, for example, the methodology of a faith-based reconciliation seminar has brought such identity-based groups as Kashmiri Muslims, Kashmiri pandits, Dogras of Jammu, and Ladakhi Buddhists together. Sitting in the same small groups, they have shared their life journeys and core values with each other. They have engaged in dialogue, acknowledged their areas of hostility, learned conflict resolution skills, discussed the sharing of privilege, apologized to each other or extended forgiveness, and had an honest conversation about their history. The graduates of the seminars are encouraged to be civic diplomats, to be intentional about reaching outside of their own identity-based group to establish relationships with other people groups. They are encouraged to begin cell groups that bring people from various identity-based groups together in a more intimate environment.

A peace accord is the capstone of bringing an end to the hostilities and establishing the political arrangements that enable two diverse people groups to understand the basis and boundaries for living together. The peace process assumes that communication is at the heart of the cause and resolution of conflict. Unless two parties can communicate with each other in a constructive, creative, and respectful manner, there is little hope of resolving the issues or restoring the relationships. One such communication tool is the learning conversation, a concept created by Douglas Stone, Bruce Patton, and Sheila Heen in their book, *Difficult Conversations*. Stone et al. describe a difficult conversation as "Anytime we feel vulnerable or our self esteem is implicated, when the issues at stake are important and the outcome uncertain, when we care deeply about what is being discussed or about the people with whom we are discussing it, there is potential for us to experience the conversation as difficult."

Stone, Patton and Heen point out that a learning conversation is, in reality, three conversations. The first element is the "What Happened? Conversation," where the parties focus on their perceptions of the truth, their assessments of intentions and impact, and their contributions to the problem. The second element is the "Feelings Conversation," which enables parties to surface the unexpressed feelings, which are at the heart of the matter. Violent long-term conflict between identity-based groups usually fosters intense hostility and antagonism, which needs to be given proper expression. At the same time, venting of strong negative feelings needs to be managed, or it can destroy the mediation and make negotiations much more difficult if not impossible. The third element is the "Identity Conversation," which means that the parties are challenged to look honestly at their perceptions of themselves. Stone et al. write, "Our anxiety results not just from having to face the other person, but having to face ourselves. The conversation may pose a threat to our identity, the story we tell ourselves about ourselves."

Stone, Patton and Heen state that one goal of a learning conversation is to create the "third story." As such, the third story is one that descries the problem in nonjudgmental terms as a difference between parties. A second goal is to create resonance between the parties. Jay Rothman in his book *Resolving Identity-Based Conflicts* writes, "When disputants interactively begin to go beneath the surface of their own reality and articulate the deep needs and values that are at stake for them in the conflict, exactly what matters so much, an underlying resonance is often discovered." A third goal is that it allows "identity quakes" to occur when parties hear themselves described in unflattering terms. This enables the parties to complexify their identities by incorporating both noble and baser qualities into a constructive and redemptive statement of truth. A fourth goal is to allow the parties to consider the effect of their past actions on each other and the need for collective acknowledgement and apology. A fifth goal is that it enables the parties to surface antagonism, vent anger, and mistrust so as to move beyond victimhood to volition and constructive exploration of options.

In utilizing the faith-based learning conversation model for mediating a conflict and arriving at a peace accord, the faith-based actor follows five basic steps:

1. Sharing life journeys and building common ground.
2. Sharing perceptions of the conflict or problem.
3. Engaging in a problem-solving approach, utilizing a faith-based reconciliation paradigm to address the particular conflict or problem.
4. Sharing where each has experienced and caused offense to the other.
5. Exploring each community's narrative of history and perception of historical wounds.

At the root of many identity-based conflicts is systemic injustice that is manifested in violations of human rights, religious persecution, lack of respect, inequity, or favoritism. A cardinal rule that I learned from my friends in the black community of South Africa is that there can be no reconciliation without justice. You cannot build a reconciled society on a foundation of injustice. Hence, an important aspect of conflict resolution seen thru a reconciliation lens is addressing and confronting areas of injustice in the systems and structures. However, from a faith-based perspective this involves more than transformation of systems and structures, it also involves transformation of hearts and relationships between the powerful and the powerless. One of the long-term issues of social justice in Europe involves both the Gypsies and the Muslims, two outcast groups in many European societies. More than simply changing systems and structures, how will hearts and relationships be transformed between mainstream Germans and Turkish Muslims of Berlin or Czechs and Gypsies of Bohemia?

The pursuit of social justice must be linked with communal political forgiveness. It is communal forgiveness that enables conflicting parties to have any future together. Parties in conflict can wax eloquently about their own suffering and can recount in excruciating detail the sins and offenses of the other party. An important part of the healing process is when the parties can realize their own culpability and acknowledge the suffering caused to the other party. When this results in apologies and forgiveness, it releases a powerful dynamic of healing in the relationship in restoring each other's humanity. Our reconciliation seminar includes a service of reconciliation, where on many occasions we have witnessed public collective apologies and the extension of forgiveness. These acts occur as a result of changed hearts, the key to resolving identity-based conflict.

Deep historical wounds that remain unhealed can cause communities and nations to become captive to a bitter history and unable to live in peace with others. Cynical political, religious, or social movement leaders are able to manipulate people by reopening old wounds. In our seminars in Kashmir, there have been honest conversations about history and attempts to identify the greatest wounds in their history. Reconciliation ceremonies can bring together the offenders and victims at the site of the offense to recall and acknowledge the offense, to apologize and extend forgiveness, which serves as a powerful symbol in forging a healed relationship.

Finally, a faith-based actor draws upon certain spiritual practices in the pursuit of reconciliation. One such tool that arises out of the building of personal relationships with the conflicting parties is the practice of a spiritual conversation, which is hardly a traditional tool of statecraft, even in unofficial settings. These conversations engage leaders in conversations of the heart—in which they share what they have suffered, their hopes, their dreams, their sorrows, their family, and their spiritual needs. Political and military leaders are often surprised to find themselves in such conversations, but they do elicit empathy and friendship. On one occasion, I brought up the subject of forgiveness in a conversation with a prominent Kashmiri separatist leader, and he responded with a forty-five-minute rant detailing his suffering. Upon finishing, he looked up at us. I thanked him for trusting us enough to share his personal pain. He responded that we were the first people who seemed to care enough to listen to his suffering. He later acknowledged that both he and his people would need to practice forgiveness if Kashmir was to have any future.

Prayer and fasting is a practice of most faith traditions. Expressing the believer's submission to God, prayer and fasting usher a spiritual power into the site of a violent conflict, one that effects a personal transformation, which conflict resolution methods and other principles cannot alone bring about. Our work in Kashmir commonly involves a team of people who pray and fast during seminars, diplomatic meetings, and public forums. No scientific methodology can test the impact of such practices, but certain episodes of transformation in our experience such as a deeply embittered person coming to a point of forgiveness toward the offender bear the marks of the sort of divine assistance that comes as a response to prayer and fasting.

Rituals and ceremonies that are normally directed toward worship, celebration, mourning, remembrance, and healing can be redirected toward the resolution of conflict and the transformation of people wounded by political violence. The reading of sacred texts, common prayer, liturgy, and rites of healing can all become tools for the faith-based actor in conflict resolution. The most poignant moments of our work in Kashmir come in a reconciliation service at the close of the seminar. With the participants seated in a circle, sacred scriptures about reconciliation are read. Participants then take the opportunity to write on a slip of paper any memories of which they want to unburden themselves—whether through apology, forgiveness, or general healing. Next, while the group is carrying out prayer and meditation, some of the participants will rise and speak words of healing. Often a member of the opposing community will then reciprocate with an acknowledgement and further words of healing. Typically, the participants close the ritual with songs of peace, including "We Shall Overcome" sung in Urdu.

Spiritual conversations, prayer and fasting, and the use of rituals are three tools available to the faith-based actor seeking to be a peacemaker. In conclusion, then, peacemaking is the third core value of faith-based reconciliation, and the means to its implementation is faith-based forms of conflict analysis and modes of intervention.

Chapter Six

SEEKING THE COMMON GOOD
THE PRINCIPLE OF SOCIAL JUSTICE

Faith-based social justice means that we seek the common good through transformation of the soul of a community.

At the age of twelve, I discovered my first passion in life—politics. Over the course of the next ten years, I came to love the rough and tumble world of hardball politics. I walked precincts, knocked on doors to register voters, campaigned with local candidates in shopping centers, and began to dream about a career in national politics. Although my parents had been lifelong blue-collar Democrats, I chose the Republican Party as my own. I was attracted by the conservative political philosophy. Having also been an accomplished debater in high school, I could adroitly argue with passion the rationale and merits of the conservative cause. During all those years, I smugly dismissed the idea of social justice as the misguided preoccupation of liberals and campus radicals. As such, I had neatly compartmentalized it under the aegis of left-wing Democratic politics. However, three things happened that profoundly changed my understanding and appreciation for the place of social justice and its relationship to a moral vision of faith-based reconciliation. First, by spring 1972, my passion for politics had turned into complete disillusionment: with myself, with fellow politicians, and with the world of politics itself. Second, in October 1972, I surrendered my life to God, and it changed my heart. Previously, I had never taken Bible reading seriously, but I found myself beginning to devour the contents of the Bible. In my reading, particularly the Jewish prophets, I discovered that contrary to my own understanding, that social justice had little to do with left-wing Democratic politics and everything to do with the heart of God. Third, in 1984, I lived for several months in South Africa near Pretoria. My family and I went there on sabbatical at the invitation of Africa Enterprise of South Africa and the Anglican Diocese of Pretoria. While there, my eyes were opened to the cruel nature of racism that I had been blind to in my own country. I witnessed firsthand, a cruel and evil regime, buttressed by the state church—use of terror, torture, and intimidation to preserve group privilege for the white Afrikaner minority. For the first time in my life, my heart was cut to ribbons by the suffering of people, and I found a certain anger rising up in my heart toward the perpetrators of injustice and toward the cruel system of white privilege that existed there. My friends in the black community would say, "There can be no reconciliation without justice." Over the course of the past twenty years in such places as Bosnia, Kosovo, Kashmir, Sudan, and, yes, America, I have come to see the profound truth of those words.

In 1993, I was part of a group that formed in the Santa Barbara community that became known as Pastors Pursuing Racial Reconciliation. Those three years were incredibly painful as I had to wrestle with destructive consequences of institutional white privilege in America, destructive to the dignity of my friends in the African American community, destructive to African American families, and destructive to my own soul as an unwitting beneficiary of white privilege. During one of our sessions, a fellow pastor told the story of President Abraham Lincoln being asked if he believed that God was on the side of the North or the South in the Civil War. Lincoln replied that he believed that the Civil War was God's judgment on the nation for the sin of slavery. If that be true, then social justice begins from a moral basis.

Faith-based social justice flows from an understanding that there is a moral grain to the universe, that there are divinely revealed values that govern human relationships and structures. As the Abrahamic tradition understands it, God has revealed his vision for how people are to live together in the political order with norms that govern their conduct. This is an essential part of a moral vision that undergirds the political, social, economic, and cultural structures of a society. Whether it is called Torah, the Sermon on the Mount, Sharia, or Dharma, God reveals an absolute basis for political community. Not only is there a moral basis for political community, but justice is an inviolate part of it.

Faith-based social justice transcends political philosophy and asks the question, "What is the common good?" Jesus of Nazareth taught the principle of faith-based social justice in his preaching about the Kingdom of God. According to Jesus, the Kingdom or Reign of God was the establishment of God's new society on earth. He taught that God's sovereign rule would establish the common good: a society based on respect for the dignity of every human being, the economics of compassion, the politics of love, the power of truth, and stewardship embodied in voluntary sacrifice. Jesus also taught that such a society could not be truly realized without transformation of that society's soul.

In the Jewish tradition, it was recognized that the greatest threat to the common good was individual and collective human sin, which was embodied in the human tendency to hoard privilege for oneself or one's people group. Hence, the hoarding of privilege was not the peculiar trait of any one identity-based group but rather an inevitable result of our human nature. Toward this end, there grew up in Hebrew society a strong prophetic voice and a moral conscience that cried out for righteousness and justice. The great Jewish prophets such as Isaiah, Jeremiah, Amos, and Micah thundered against the gross violations of God's sovereign rule by the existence of oppression, exploitation, and tyranny. As such, the prophetic message assured both individual and collective accountability to God under a standard of social justice. As we read in Micah 6:8, "He has showed you O man, what is good. And what does the Lord require of you? To act justly and to love mercy and to walk humbly with your God." Muhammed, in seventh century Arabia, encountered a society in transition that was steeped in not only polytheism but also in materialism and social injustice. According to the Qu'ran, the Abrahamic tradition embodies a moral vision of social justice at the heart of the social order and as the basis for *ummah* or community. In Surah 16:90 we read, "God commands justice, the doing of good, and liberality to kith and kin, and He forbids all shameful deeds, and injustice and rebellion; He instructs you, that ye may receive admonition." In the Hindu tradition, Swami Dayananda Saraswati, founder of a nineteenth-century reform movement, laid down social action as one of the ten principles for Hindus to follow. The establishment of ashrams were intended to be small-scale versions of a classless society based on social justice. Mahatma Gandhi's political philosophy of *sarvodaya* (universal welfare) and *loksangraha* (common good) were derived from the sacred texts and were important contributions to contemporary sociopolitical thought. In the Buddhist tradition, the disciples of the Buddha were taught that social justice is an expression of the politics of compassion (karuna).

Let us now take a closer look at the constituent elements that embody the common good in a society. First of all, the common good flows from an understanding that all human beings are created in the image or attributes of God and are, therefore, worthy of respect and dignity. Respect, as a foundation of social justice, is part of what Aristotle would define as "our due," what human beings owe to each other. God gave the Ten Commandments to Moses as the essence or core of a moral law, and they can be summarized in one word: respect. Respect for God, respect for one another, and respect for one another's property is a foundation of faith-based social justice. In our faith-based reconciliation seminars, we discover that respect emerges as a common core value desired on the individual level. However, when that same core value is applied to describe behavior of institutions as a collective entity, it ranks very low or is nonexistent. Hence, it should be no surprise at the level of disrespect within both the Episcopal Church and American mainstream culture. Those outside of the United States experience it in terms of our bullying behavior.

Human rights flow from an understanding that human beings are created in the image or attributes of God and are worthy of respect and dignity. Human rights are a complex set of freedoms given by God, preserved by the state, and exercised for the common good. Human rights are conferred on an individual by a sovereign God, not the state. The state is simply a human vehicle for the preservation of our human rights. Hence, the state has no authority to confer human rights but will be held accountable by God based on whether or not it has preserved its citizen's human rights. The concept of the state having a divine function to protect and to serve its citizens is a foreign concept to people who have lived under conditions of long-term systemic injustice, particularly where the security services have been utilized to repress their legitimate aspirations.

Human rights are not only given by God and preserved by the state, but they must be exercised for the common good. The sacred texts teach the principle of mutual submission, which means that in the exercise of one's human rights, a person must take into account the rights and needs of others. An individual cannot exercise his rights without considering their consequences on others. The right to freedom of speech must respect the safety or dignity of others. This, of course, raises the question of the balance between rights and responsibilities.

People of goodwill can disagree on the scope of human rights. Certainly most people would agree on such rights as freedom of religion, thought, expression, speech, life, movement, and association. Freedom to make moral choices, to develop our human potential, and to choose our vocation. Freedom from terror, torture, and abuse. However, some would include as human rights: food, shelter, clothing, or employment. Others might disagree. The boundaries of human rights seem debatable, but the principle is not, because it is the outward manifestation of respect, of being given our due. This is why Mahatma Gandhi, because of his understanding of respect for the dignity of every human being, sought not only to free India from British rule but also to empower the masses to shape their destiny. This also led him to practice nonviolence (ahimsa) through fasting as a method of purification so his disciples could resist the impulse of violence.

Second, the common good flows from the practice of the economics of compassion. The Abrahamic tradition teaches that each family should have a permanent stake in economic life. Since the family is the basic unit of every society, it should be able to share in economic opportunity. Equity, which is one aspect of the economics of compassion, involves concepts of fairness and sharing. Equity involves equality of opportunity but cannot guarantee equality of outcome. Hence, the sacred texts clearly condemn the use of economic power to exploit others and exhorts the leaders of a community to remedy economic injustices. Mahatma Gandhi, in his bid to empower the masses, sought to encourage the development of small businesses and utilization of indigenous resources such as salt and cotton. Gandhi wanted all the people of India to have an economic stake in the community, and he also sought to avoid shifting power from one set of rulers (the British) to another set of rulers (wealthy and politically powerful Indians). In an ironic way, the forces of globalization may bring about by market forces what we have failed to do through compassion: shifting jobs and economic opportunity to the global South as new economic development zones spring up in Bangalore, Shanghai, Mexico, and Brazil.

Third, the common good flows from the practice of the politics of love. In the chapter on "Demolishing Walls of Hostility: The Principle of Inclusion," I explained the nature and challenge of the politics of love. Here, I will consider its application as it relates to faith-based social justice. It is significant to bear in mind that in the Islamic worldview there is an integrated approach to the religious and political realms. In other words, the two must be held in creative tension. The politics of love involves a desire for the well-being of all groups of people in a society, caring for the needs of each other, and allowing for the possibility of redressing wrongs. Hence, the politics of love seeks social virtue above sectional interest.

Impartiality, which is one aspect of the politics of love, challenges our human tendency to design systems that favor ourselves and our people group. Much of the cynicism that common people have about politics and politicians is that it usually means favoritism for one group of people and discrimination against another group. Favoritism is showing unmerited partiality toward a person, group, or nation and is a natural human construction that derives from our broken or fallen nature. That is why most revolutions fail to produce genuine social justice for the masses. Generally, one group of privileged elites is thrown out of power and is replaced by a new ruling class. In almost every state that adopted the Marxist moral vision in the twentieth century, there was a failure to achieve true social justice. Privilege was reserved for the ruling Communist Party members while the masses were repressed by a harsh state apparatus that utilized fear, terror, and torture.

The politics of love must also consider the relationship between the individual and the state. The state is a tangible political entity—which has sovereignty, territory, population, diplomatic recognition, internal organization, internal loyalty, and symbols. From another perspective, a state is also a group of individuals—which actually runs a nation by making its laws, establishing policy, punishing those who violate the law, and acquiring the money to run the machinery of the state. As such, the state possesses a monopoly of legal coercive power. The state differs from civil society. Society is marked by the voluntary character of its associations. The state is characterized by the use of force. Thomas Hobbes in *Leviathan* wrote that the state, through the social contract, receives the right to use violence in return for extending security. This creates four possible scenarios with respect to the relationship between the individual and the state. The first scenario would be anarchism, which is an absence of the state. Is it possible that anarchy could embody the politics of love? Could social justice even be achieved in a system that has no boundaries or structures? The sacred texts would seem to make a strong case that a governing authority is part of the divine provision to protect us from the baser instincts of our human nature. In the New Testament, people of faith are actually exhorted to pray for those in authority so that all might live in peace and security. The second scenario is the minimal state wherein the state apparatus is limited to the minimal amount necessary to assure individual freedom. This scenario limits the state to three basic functions: protection from foreign invasion, protection of the rights of its citizens, and judging in conflicts between individuals. In this scenario, social justice is achieved by individuals exhibiting attributes of love and mercy. The third scenario is the maximal state, which provides a more intrusive state apparatus in the belief that it will promote the well-being of all in the society. It views the state as a positive, benevolent vehicle for promoting social justice and grants the state whatever powers are needed to bring about that objective. The fourth scenario is totalitarianism, which is total control of the individual by the state. This scenario asserts that the individual is nothing while the state is everything. Some of the more extreme examples include fascist Germany during the 1930s and 1940s, the Marxist Eastern Bloc countries between 1950 and 1990, and Afghanistan under the Taliban during the 1990s. Is it possible that totalitarianism could embody the politics of love? Ask the six million Jewish victims who perished under Nazi Germany. Ask the forty million victims that perished in Stalinist Russia. Ask the two million victims that perished under the Khmer Rouge in Cambodia.

One key issue in social justice is the role of the state in fostering social justice. To what extent is social justice to be achieved by the advocacy of individuals and groups within the context of the minimal state or by the coercive powers of the state within the context of the maximal state? People of faith, who embody different political philosophies, disagree over this very issue. Nevertheless, the sacred texts seem to suggest that the politics of love, as embodied in faith-based social justice, can only be realized within the context of the minimal/maximal state that involves a complex interplay of civil society advocacy and state intervention on behalf of minority communities.

Fourth, the common good flows from the power of truth. Mahatma Gandhi had a lifelong commitment to truth. For Gandhi, the concept of *satya* or truth-force was at the heart of nonviolent resistance. Jesus of Nazareth taught his disciples that if they would adhere to his teaching that they would know the truth and that the truth would set them free. In spite of its possible flaws, the South African Truth and Reconciliation Commission sought to bring evil and wrongdoing by the state out into the open so that the truth could be known by all. Injustice, oppression, and tyranny flourish in a climate of secrecy. The powers of darkness are at their best when they can hide behind the veil of national security or state secrets. Truth is the enemy of injustice because when evil human behavior, either individual or collective, is brought into the light of public knowledge and scrutiny, it leads to accountability, guilt and shame for the perpetrator, and freedom for the victims. Hence, truth is inseparable from faith-based social justice. However, like Pontius Pilate we might ask the question that he asked of Jesus, "What is truth?" It is illuminating that the state (Pilate) turns to the faith community (Jesus) for an answer to that question. Perhaps, this suggests a unique role for the faith community in every society, being a prophetic voice and moral conscience, particularly in relationship to civil authority.

The leaders of the American Civil Rights Movement referred to this as speaking truth to power. As such, the prophetic voice is a most unwelcome and yet a most necessary voice in every society but especially in the corridors of power. However, how does a community discern the authentic prophetic voice in contradistinction to the political agenda of a particular party or lobby? Perhaps one way that truth can surface in the political realm is through civic forums, where divergent interests and views are forced to find common ground. The Jewish prophet Jeremiah specifically warned the people of Israel against false prophets, those individuals who sought to speak on behalf of God or appeal to a higher moral authority and yet had not stood in the councils of the Lord. In other words, a false prophet was one who spoke without any divine authority or power. As a friend of mine, Francis Maguire, is fond of asking, "Why is it that conservatives seem to focus only on liberal demons, and liberals seem to focus only on conservative demons?" People of faith must genuinely wrestle with discerning the authentic prophetic voice derived from transcendent motivation as opposed to that which emanates from the seductive voices of postmodern relativism. It must truly be a hellish nightmare for policy makers and leaders of the state to hear the authentic voice of moral authority above the cacophonous clamoring of special interests cloaked in the rhetoric of the common good.

So how does a community recognize the authentic prophetic voice? First of all, the authentic prophetic voice is in harmony with the moral grain of the universe, and it seeks to call the community back to embrace God's original moral vision as embodied in the sacred texts. Through a process of truth telling and dream sharing, it calls the leaders and the people to a genuine repentance that means turning away from oppression, exploitation, or tyranny. In this context, the element of hope also emerges because the prophetic voice seeks to contextualize the specter of accountability within the framework of God's love for creation and God's greater purpose of *tikkun olam*, of healing, repair, and transformation. Secondly, the authentic prophetic voice flows from the prophet's intimacy with God. How can one possibly know the heart of the divine if one has not cultivated an intimate relationship? One overlooked aspect of the lives of individuals such as Mahatma Gandhi, Rosa Parks, Martin Luther King Jr., and Caesar Chavez was their deep spirituality, their submission to the will of God. Their prophetic voices and actions resonated so deeply because they flowed from intimacy with God. Thirdly, the authentic prophetic voice assumes God's sovereign rule over a society that seeks the common good. The prophet knows that there can be no true social justice in a society that casts aside the idea of accountability to God or that is not committed to the common good. The prophetic voice can only be heard and heeded in a context, where these two values are part of the foundation or moral vision of the society. I dare say that if India had been ruled by Nazi Germany instead of Great Britain, Mahatma Gandhi might have met a very different fate. Finally, the authentic prophetic voice assumes the unhappy burden of pointing to the bleached bones of the society or nation that refused to listen to God. Martin Luther King Jr. sometimes warned that it was possible to be too late in doing the right thing. Through much of the nineteenth century in America, there were prophetic voices warning about the moral consequences of slavery. Those voices went largely unheeded, and, by 1861, it became too late. The American Civil War broke out pitting brothers against each other, one of the darkest chapters in American history. Prior to World War II, a Confessing Church movement sprung up in Germany and warned German Christians against the evils of the Nazi ideology and regime. However, on September 1, 1939, it became too late. People of faith in Germany had refused to listen to such prophetic voices as Dietrich Bonhoeffer and Martin Niemoeller. Ultimately, they saw their nation destroyed by allied bombing, occupied by the victorious allies, and saddled with the shame of historical guilt.

Fifth, the common good flows from stewardship embodied in voluntary sacrifice. The teaching of Jesus of Nazareth was embodied not only in his words but in the example of his life. The Gospel of John tells us how at the Last Supper with his followers that he took up a washbasin and towel and washed their feet. He then said to them, "Do you understand what I have done for you? You call me teacher and Lord and rightly so, for that is what I am. Now that I, your Lord and teacher, have washed your feet, you also should wash one another's feet. I have set you an example that you should do as I have done for you." The Western system of liberal democracy and free market capitalism is grounded in the enlightenment notion of enlightened self-interest. In other words, it assumes that human nature will lead an individual to put his or her own interests ahead of others but within a context of submitting to the common good. This is the assumption behind the philanthropic impulse, which seeks to activate individual and corporate generosity for the benefit of all in society but particularly toward caring for the most vulnerable members: the poor, the handicapped, the women, the children, and the elderly. However, Jesus did not appeal to enlightened self-interest. He modeled a life of stewardship embodied in self-sacrifice. He spoke about the need to die to self. Mahatma Gandhi was convinced that social transformation could never be truly achieved through any amount of ideological propaganda, terrorist intimidation, or wholesale persecution. It could only be achieved by following the example of Jesus of Nazareth, who emptied himself of personal ambition and took on the attitude and actions of a servant. Stewardship means that the center of gravity of our life is not self-actualization but self-sacrifice. Enlightened self-interest, no matter how it is cast, is still grounded in self-interest: preserving personal and group privilege.

Privilege is favor or opportunity that comes to us, sometimes earned and sometimes unearned. It arises out of ancestry, gender, family, social ties, education, political connections, or wealth. Privilege opens doors and creates possibilities for individuals and groups. It is human nature that the powerful group in a society designs the system to preserve privilege for itself. This confers advantage on one group and disadvantage on another group. The sacred texts teach us that the hoarding of privilege is a sin and will ultimately bring about divine judgment on that society. The harshest words of the sacred texts are reserved for those who hoard privilege. The key to social justice is the sharing of privilege, which can be a nonzero-sum exchange. Gain for one group does not have to result in loss for another group. This occurs as we attempt to "expand the pie" and create opportunities through advocacy, which is probably one of the most significant ways of embodying voluntary self-sacrifice; and it takes on two forms: social service and social action on behalf of the most vulnerable elements of a society.

As a white male Christian, I have come to realize through honest and painful conversations with women, ethnic, and religious minorities in America the extent to which I have benefited and continue to benefit from a system of white privilege. Those of us in majority communities tend to be oblivious to our status. As such, my commitment to faith-based social justice is to expand the pie by creating and contributing to opportunities and access for women and minority communities. A side of me struggles against that by preserving the status quo. Another side of me recognizes that change will benefit all by creating a society more consistent with the divine moral vision.

The final point I would like to make about faith-based social justice is how it is achieved: through transforming of the community's soul. In the sacred texts, the soul of a community, a collective entity, is comprised of five elements: systems, structures, relationships, hearts, and principalities. *Systems* are the philosophical foundations or moral vision of a society that express the core values, worldview, and rationale for its corporate life. *Structures* embody the outward organization of a society that enables it to carry out its essential functions. *Relationships* involve the complex interplay of socialization, voluntary association, intimacy, and power sharing. It is in the realm of relationships that the dynamics of collective identity assert themselves and govern how we define "us" vs. "them." *Hearts* involve the volitional dynamics that balance the tension between seeking the common good as opposed to individual or group interest. *Principalities* are those spiritual entities that shape the governing dynamics of a society and influence its ability to embrace or reject God's sovereign rule. Secular models of social justice typically focus only on systemic and structural change and overlook the need to transform relationships between the powerful and the powerless, to change the hearts of people engaged in or supporting injustice, and to overcome the spiritual forces of darkness that sustain the hording of privilege.

Faith-based social justice is distinguished by its emphasis on transforming the soul of a community. It recognizes, first of all, as many American Civil Rights leaders of the 1960s came to realize, that it is not enough to change the racism embedded in systems and structures of white privilege. One must change the racism embedded in human hearts and relationships. One must also recognize, as Martin Luther King Jr. did, that the outward manifestation of social injustice is social and political. However, the root of injustice is spiritual. It is a spiritual force of demonic origin that seeks to sow seeds of division through an emphasis on group interest and privilege rather than the common good.

The transformation of the soul of a community may require public human activities such as protest marches, strikes, fasts, community forums, and legislative activity to overturn unjust structures or create new avenues of privilege. However, it also requires the quiet, private building of relationships between those who exercise power and those who are the most vulnerable members of a society. It reminds us of the old adage that says, "It is not what you know, but who you know." Transforming the soul of a community also involves prophetic voices touching the moral consciences of the privileged group that leads to genuine repentance on their part: a change of heart leading to changed thinking, leading to changed behavior. Transforming the soul of a community also involves spiritual renewal through divine intervention that converts people's hearts and motivates them to overturn systemic injustice and seek God's ancient vision for the political order and civil society. It recognizes that, more often than not, the greatest barrier to the common good is not unjust structures but hardened hearts.

In conclusion, social justice is the fourth core value of faith-based reconciliation, and the means to implementation is transforming the soul of a community that leads to the common good.

Chapter Seven

HEALING RELATIONSHIPS
BETWEEN INDIVIDUALS AND COMMUNITIES
THE PRINCIPLE OF FORGIVENESS

Forgiveness means that we exercise forgiveness and repentance as individuals and communities to create the possibility of a better future together.

During a faith-based reconciliation seminar in Kashmir in June 2001, I was teaching about the principle of forgiveness. At the end of the presentation, one participant, a Kashmiri Muslim, stood up to ask a question. He pointed a finger at me and asked, "Are you saying that we must forgive the Indian authorities and give up the struggle for justice? Does reconciliation mean capitulation or compromise?" I replied to him that extending forgiveness did not mean giving up a nonviolent struggle for justice. However, it is forgiveness that makes the difference between pursuing justice or revenge. I asked him, "Is it justice or revenge that you seek? If it is justice, then you have no choice but to forgive the Indian authorities; otherwise, no matter how noble your words, it is really revenge that you seek."

To be created in the image or attributes of God means that we are social beings designed to live in relationship with other human beings. In the second chapter of Genesis, God says of Adam, "It is not good for him to be alone." As such, faith-based reconciliation recognizes the importance and centrality of human relationships. One of the strongest human impulses is to seek out intimacy with others. "To know and to be known," brings the deepest human satisfaction. At the same time, the most compelling evidence of our fallen human nature is the alienation, pain, brokenness, and failure we experience in relationships. All of us can point to broken relationships in our lives. Whether between two individuals or two nations, broken relationships are a burden or yoke around the neck of the parties involved, and they weaken the fabric and vitality of the larger community. Forgiveness is the key to healing relationships because it sets the individual or community free from the burden of anger, pain, hatred, resentment, and the desire for revenge. Forgiveness is powerful because it changes lives and transforms societies by releasing them from the wounds of the past.

Jesus of Nazareth taught the principle of forgiveness. One of his followers, Simon Peter, asked him the question, "How many times shall I forgive my brother? Seven times?" Jesus replied, "You must forgive your brother seventy times seven." Jesus was teaching that forgiveness must be extended from the heart of the victim to the offender over and over until it becomes a permanent condition. As Jesus hung on the cross, he cried out "Father, forgive them, for they know not what they are doing." These words of Jesus, "Father forgive," are enshrined in the stones of Coventry Cathedral in England and represent a faith-based response to the German bombing of the cathedral during World War II and have been the spiritual impetus to the Community of the Cross of Nails, an international ministry of reconciliation.

The Torah teaches the principle of forgiveness in two powerful encounters between brothers. Esau and Jacob, two sons of Isaac, were separated and estranged for many years over Jacob's stealing of Esau's birthright as the eldest son. The period of separation had caused a sense of dread within Jacob about the eventual meeting between the two of them. At the same time, it had created a sense of repentance within his heart and a desire to make amends to his brother. During that same period, God had enabled Esau to forgive Jacob so that when they encountered each other, Esau ran to embrace his brother, and they were reconciled.

Joseph was one of the twelve sons of Jacob. One day, he had a dream, which seemed to suggest eventual preeminence over his brothers. When he shared the dream with his brothers, their reaction was predictably negative. At first, they sought to kill him but changed their minds and sold him to some Midianite merchants who, in turn, sold him to one of pharaoh's officials in Egypt. A period of servitude led to a false accusation and imprisonment. However, his ability to interpret dreams brought him favor in pharaoh's eyes and eventually he rose from the status of prisoner to the position of prime minister of Egypt. A subsequent famine throughout the Middle East sent his brothers on a journey to Egypt to procure food. Initially, they did not recognize their brother Joseph, but later the brothers received the shock of their life when Joseph revealed his identity, and it led to a process of reconciliation at the heart of which was Joseph's forgiveness of his brothers for their malicious action in selling him to the Midianite merchants. Joseph had been able to forgive them because had to come to see that God's greater purpose had been served even through the evil actions of his brothers.

In the Qu'ran, Surah 59:10, it provides a sobering admonition that if the person of faith expects forgiveness from God, they must be willing to bestow it on others. Furthermore, the Qu'ran teaches that one of the names and attributes of God is All Forgiving, Most Merciful" (Surah 24:22). Muhammed embodied this teaching in his act of forgiveness toward his enemies in Mecca. In the Hindu tradition, the *Mahabharata* tells the ancient story of a conversation between Prahlad and Vali that explores the merits of forgiveness versus might. In the Buddhist tradition, the practice of loving kindness is embodied in the act of forgiveness. In the Sikh tradition, forgiveness is described in the *Granth Sahib* as love at its highest power. In essence, no one religious tradition can claim an exclusive franchise on the concept of forgiveness. The process of repentance, apology, and forgiveness is a universal truth available to everyone everywhere.

We shall now consider six elements in the process of healing relationships whether between individuals or between communities. Three elements represent actions that must be taken by the victim: forgiveness, redeeming the violence, and burden bearing. Three elements represent actions that must be taken by the offender: repentance, confession/apology, and restitution.

The first element in the healing of a relationship is forgiveness, which must be extended by the victim and received by the offender. According to its ancient Greek roots, the meaning of the word "forgiveness" is the following:

> To release from liability to suffer punishment or penalty; to let go, release or remit; and to cancel a debt in full. To cancel a debt in full means that you absorb the liability someone else deserves to pay. Forgiveness means to bestow favor freely or unconditionally that is undeserved and cannot be earned.

Forgiveness releases both the victim and the offender from an interdependent bondage. It releases the victim from his/her hurt and the offender from his/her guilt. Forgiveness is an act of the will, not the emotions. If I wait until I feel forgiving toward someone, I will never forgive him or her. It is first and foremost a volitional action. I forgive because I choose to do so, not because I feel forgiving toward them. Many times, we become mired in unforgiveness because we are waiting to feel forgiving toward the offender. Forgiveness is unilateral. It is not dependent on the actions or response of the other party. Jesus taught in the New Testament that we are to forgive regardless of the response of the other party. You are ultimately responsible only for your own actions in a broken relationship. Sometimes, because of the choices of the other party, it is not possible to completely reconcile a relationship. Forgiveness, on your part, may be all that can reasonably happen at a particular moment. However, don't give up the possibility of a future change of heart in the other party. Some years ago, I found myself in a situation of needing to forgive a colleague for his actions, which contributed significantly to our inability to continue working together. One morning, after I had relocated to a new situation, I was out walking and praying and came to the heartfelt conviction that I needed to forgive this person. I didn't feel like forgiving him. I wanted to hold on to my anger and my sense of victimhood. I didn't want to give up my feelings of moral superiority. However, the words of Jesus echoed in the background, "If you do not forgive your brother from your heart, your heavenly Father will not forgive you." I gulped, and then I prayed for the first time, "Lord God, I forgive this person from my heart. Help my unforgiveness." I would like to say that I heard angels in heaven singing, but I didn't. I would like to say that I felt this immediate emotional and spiritual release, but I didn't. I would like to say that the two of us were immediately reconciled, but I can't. But it was the first step of a prayer I prayed many times before I felt genuine forgiveness toward him, and the situation opened up for the possibility of a reconciliation meeting between us.

Forgiveness must become a permanent attitude. Jesus taught in the New Testament that we must forgive over and over until it becomes a permanent attitude of the heart. Forgiveness is not a passive process of forgetting or excusing. It is an active process of remembering and pardoning. Forgiveness does not automatically release the wrongdoer from the consequences of their actions. An offender might still have to face civil or criminal penalties for their actions or consider appropriate forms of restitution to the victim. In the Parable of the Prodigal Son, the father reassures the elder brother that "all I have is yours." The prodigal son had taken his share earlier. The father's forgiveness did not change that. In 1981, when Mehmet Ali Aga shot Pope John Paul II, the pope went to see him in prison and extended forgiveness to him for his actions. Nevertheless, it did not release Mehmet Ali Aga from having to remain in prison.

The second element in the healing of a relationship is an outgrowth of the decision by the victim to forgive the offender. This involves redeeming the violence, wherein the victim embarks on a process of allowing God and the community to restore his/her humanity. Political prisoners from the communist era in the former Eastern Bloc, young Kashmiris tortured by Indian security services or maimed for life by militant groups, orphans in Rwanda and Burundi, and Afghani women surviving Taliban rule are just the tip of the iceberg of the violence perpetrated in the name of God, nation, tribe, or simply naked greed. What does it mean to redeem violence and suffering?

> Redeeming violence is a spiritual, moral, and emotional process that enables a victim to recover the basic elements of their humanity—which has been stripped from them through an act or acts of violence by individuals, militant groups, or the state. The basic elements of our humanity include our identity, our sense of security, and our ability to trust.

Violence is the physical, emotional, or moral violation of our person and/or our property. Types of violence include verbal abuse, spousal battery, rape, incest, robbery, war, torture, racism, or hate crimes. Violence strips us of our humanity by destroying our dignity, our personhood or our bodily integrity, and, hence, our identity. It reveals our vulnerability and destroys our sense of security. It undermines our ability to trust people, the authorities or our way of life.

The redeeming process consists of four elements. The first element is "crying out" as the victim gives voice to their pain. The second element is justice for the victim, wherein the offender is held accountable and is willing to make restitution to the victim. The third element is bringing the truth into the light, wherein the truth of what has been done to the victim is spoken of openly and acknowledged by the offender. The fourth element is the reconstruction of the victim's memory of the event by enabling them to discover meaning and purpose in the suffering. Victor Frankl, in his study of Jewish Holocaust survivors, found that a key to both survival and recovery was discovering a sense of meaning or a greater purpose in their suffering. Over the course of thirty years as a pastor, I have provided pastoral care to adult women who had been victims of child/sexual abuse as children. It was important to spend time listening compassionately to their suffering, to help them define justice in the situation, to confront the perpetrator of the violence, to bring the truth out into the open in the family, and to discover some sort of redemptive purpose in their suffering. Each situation was unique in both its circumstances and resolution. There is no single recipe for redeeming violence. I found this was also true in listening to former political prisoners in Slovakia in the early 1990s or young Kashmiris who had been tortured by Indian security services.

The third element in the healing of a relationship, which is also an outgrowth of forgiveness, is that the victim must also be willing to bear the burden of that which cannot be changed. The human motivation for revenge is powerful, both in individuals and in communities. Many conflicts in the world today carry a dimension of settling old scores. Slobodan Milosovic may have cynically manipulated Serbs into a war of aggression against Croats, Bosnian Muslims, and Kosovar Abanians during the 1990s, because he appealed to the deep need for revenge for the suffering experienced at the hands of Ottoman Turks and the Croatian Ustasha. Around the world, there are countless alligator-infested swamps of revenge lurking in the collective hearts of communities and nations that cry out for expression.

> Burden bearing begins with a decision by the victim to surrender the desire and possibility for revenge, even if it is only in their own heart. It means accepting the painful truth that there may be certain aspects of the actions of an offender that cannot be changed or undone.

A drunk driver that strikes the victim's vehicle, killing her small child, can never bring that child back. A rapist cannot undo the profound sense of violation experienced by his victim. No amount of repentance can bring back a family member lynched by a white supremacy group. Suffice it to say that the act of burden bearing is the singularly most difficult and courageous act by a victim. Many victims give up revenge simply for personal freedom. However, sometimes the act of burden bearing can extend a grace toward the offender that is not deserved or can only come through a supernatural intervention in the heart of the victim. Burden bearing is that decisive action at the fork in the road that chooses the future path of forgiveness instead of revenge for the past. Burden bearing is what makes forgiveness possible. Hence, the person of faith clings to the teaching in the sacred texts that God can use all things—even the evil, destructive events of our life—to serve a greater purpose.

On the offender's side of the equation is the fourth element in the healing of a relationship, which is that the offender must be willing to repent for their actions. Repentance, like forgiveness, is personal to one side and doesn't demand the other's cooperation. Repentance begins with a changed heart, which results in changed thinking and, ultimately, changed behavior. No relationship can be healed if the offender continues to engage in offensive, evil, or destructive behavior. A gossip who continues to assassinate someone's character behind his or her back has not come to repentance. A community that continues to uphold group privilege has not come to repentance. A state that continues to commit human rights violations has not come to repentance.

Repentance consists of three basic elements. First, it requires a recognition by the offender that their actions were morally wrong. What they did was both an offense against God and against the victim. Second, it requires a genuine sorrow that grows from an awareness of the hurt or damage caused to the victim. Sorrow experienced by the offender just because they were caught or exposed is not true repentance and is not the basis for healing a relationship. Third, it requires a willingness to be held accountable for one's actions toward God, toward the victim, and toward the larger community. An offender who continues to shift blame for their behavior onto others or onto mitigating circumstances is clearly failing to take responsibility for their actions. When former president Bill Clinton finally acknowledged his wrongdoing in his actions with Monica Lewinski, it set off a stormy public debate. How genuine was his repentance? Was he expressing sorrow because of the damage caused to the public trust or because he was caught and had to suffer unpleasant consequences? Only Bill Clinton can truly know what was in his heart. Perhaps we will never truly know.

The fifth element in the healing of a relationship is that the offender must be willing to confess and apologize to the victim. A proper apology can be the most powerful and liberating component of healing a relationship. Yet where in our formation as children or in our education are we taught the proper form of an apology? A proper apology—whether by an individual, a community, or a sovereign state—may vary from culture to culture. Nevertheless, there are eight basic ingredients in an effective apology that seem to transcend culture:

- Acknowledgement of moral culpability: "I was wrong to have said or done . . ." This demonstrates moral character.
- Acknowledgement of the offense or wrongdoing as specifically as possible: "This is what I did . . ." The more specific you are in your apology, the more likely that you will receive a positive response.
- Acknowledgement of awareness of the impact of your behavior: "This is how I understand that it affected you . . ." This demonstrates empathy and compassion.
- Expression of sorrow or regret at having caused offense: "I feel sadness that I did this to you . . ." This demonstrates caring.

- Acknowledgement that there is no adequate or true justification for your behavior: "There is no excuse for my actions that caused you pain . . ." This demonstrates sincere godly sorrow for your actions.
- Explanation of what you will do to make restitution and/or alter your behavior in the future.
- Acknowledgement that you are prepared to accept the consequences of your actions. Avoiding consequences creates the impression that you are attempting to avoid responsibility for your actions and that your apology is insincere.
- Plea for forgiveness: "Will you forgive me?" This is the signal that you have done all you can and that the response has now been shifted to the other person.

Some years ago, I received an angry letter from a member of the congregation citing something I had said during a public worship service as the cause of his anger. At first, I felt defensive and saw his reaction as his interpretation or problem. However, as I reread the letter over and over, I began to hear my words through his heart and began to realize how my words had caused offense to him. My heart shifted from feeling defensive to feeling sorrow for the pain I had caused him. I called him up and suggested a meeting between us. As he entered my office and sat down, I could tell from his body language that he was ready for a gargantuan, take-no-prisoners fight. I began the conversation by thanking him for his honesty although it had been painful to me to face my own moral culpability. I followed this eightfold process in acknowledging my actions, apologizing, and asking for forgiveness. As I concluded, I watched the tension visibly drain from his body as he graciously forgave me and stated that he considered the matter healed and closed.

The sixth element in the healing of a relationship is that the offender must be willing to make restitution to the victim. Restitution attempts to restore or replace what the offender has damaged or destroyed. It serves both as a sign of sincerity and good faith to the victim, and it benefits society by making destructive behavior unprofitable. In addition, it restores the moral balance. The sacred texts teach that restitution is appropriate both for personal injuries of a physical or social nature and for damaged, lost, or destroyed property. Unintentional damage should involve simple restitution, wherein the offender repairs or replaces the property. However, intentional damage should involve more than simple restitution. The Jewish scriptures provide that if the offender repents before the damage was discovered, they should pay for the property plus 20 percent of its value.

When there has been intentional theft and the offender is caught with the undamaged property, he should return the property and compensate its equivalent value as well. If the offender is caught after disposing of the property, he should pay at least four times the value. If the property is difficult to replace, he should pay at least five times the value.

Sometimes the possibility or impact of restitution seems dwarfed by the enormity of the offense. How can a rapist ever adequately compensate his victim? How can a drunk driver who has killed a small child with an automobile ever replace that life? How can the German government ever begin to undo the evil of the Holocaust against European Jews and others? Nevertheless, while restitution may in some cases never be adequate to restore or replace that which has been destroyed, it is still an important expression of sincerity, repentance, and good faith on the part of the offender toward the victim. It also has important spiritual implications of restoring the moral balance in the community. In the West, the criminal justice system is increasingly adopting the principles of restorative justice, which is grounded in a faith-based philosophy in which crime is seen in terms of broken relationships or broken communal harmony rather than broken laws. One might posit that in many crimes, there is no preexisting personal relationship between the offender and the victim. In a sense, the criminal action has, in effect, created an interdependent relationship between the offender and the victim. From a restorative perspective, the offender needs the victim's forgiveness to release them from the bondage of guilt while the victim needs the offender's acknowledgement, apology, and, perhaps, restitution to restore them to wholeness. One of the essential ingredients of restorative justice is the willingness of the offender to make restitution to the victim. In the Arab-Islamic approach to conflict resolution, the process of sulh involves the payment of *diyya*, a just and symbolic compensation determined by the severity and unique damages of the case and by historical precedent. Increasingly, whole groups such as Jewish Holocaust survivors, Japanese internment camp residents, and descendants of African American slaves have sought or are seeking restitution for the evil or destructive actions of a particular state.

In conclusion, forgiveness is the fifth core value of faith-based reconciliation, and it forms the cornerstone of healing relationships between individuals and between communities.

Chapter Eight

FACING THE TRUTH ABOUT HISTORY
THE PRINCIPLE OF HEALING COLLECTIVE WOUNDS

Healing means that we seek to heal the wounds of history through acknowledgement of suffering and injustice.

In spring 1988, I traveled to Uganda with David Prior, an Anglican priest from London, for the purpose of promoting a project known as Operation Pearl. This initiative, ambitious in scope, was a faith-based effort to bring about deep healing of the spiritual, emotional, and moral trauma that ensued from the genocidal reign of Idi Amin. One evening, I was moved to tears as Anglican Archbishop Yona Okoth described for us the arrival of Amin's soldiers at his home. They crashed in the front doors of the house and rounded up all the members of his household. As the archbishop's family stood in the living room in fearful and abject silence, hands tied behind their backs, the soldiers stiffened as a second group of vehicles pulled up; and, moments later, Idi Amin himself entered the room. After verbally taunting the archbishop for over an hour, he ordered two of the soldiers to take him to a deserted place and put a bullet in his skull. The two soldiers escorted the archbishop outside the house and put him into an army jeep. They drove for almost three hours outside of Kampala toward the frontier of Kenya. Finally, they pulled off the road and led the archbishop on foot into a densely wooded forest. Ten minutes later, they stopped and ordered him to kneel at the base of a large tree. He could feel the cold metal of a revolver at the base of his neck and then hear the cocking of the trigger. Praying quietly under his breath, the archbishop waited for the end to come. After what seemed an eternity, a heavy boot pushed against his shoulder, knocking the archbishop over so that he was lying on the ground with his hands tied behind him. He could hear the soldiers running away. He waited there several hours before he got up, managed to remove the ropes, and began to walk rapidly toward the border of Kenya. Some days later, he crossed the border into freedom and exile.

As I have reflected over the years on the archbishop's story, I came to realize that it represented only the tip of the iceberg of horror and bloodshed that had left behind a deeply wounded nation. However, as my work of faith-based diplomacy has taken me to such places as Bosnia, Serbia, Kosovo, Burundi, Rwanda, Kashmir, and Sudan, I have encountered one wounded nation after another. Many times, I have asked myself, "Given this stark reality, how does this fit into any kind of coherent divine plan for the human community?"

In the Abrahamic tradition, the sacred texts reveal that God does have a plan and purpose for human history, which takes into account both human free will and the presence of evil. History is viewed as moving toward a telos or goal. In Revelation 22:2, the last chapter of the last book in the New Testament, there is a remarkable verse that graphically reminds us of the divine heart and plan for human history. In it we read, "On each side of the river stood the tree of life, bearing twelve crops of fruit, yielding its fruit every month. And the leaves of the tree are for the healing of the nations." Here, we have the essence of God's great purpose: the healing of the nations.

The concept of nation is derived from the Greek "ethnos," which means a people group who have common characteristics such as race, language, religion, culture, heritage, historical experiences, values, and regular social, political, and economic interaction. A nation is an entity that has a feeling of community or soul and a sense of distinctiveness from other people groups. In our historical and contemporary experiences, we see three distinct types of people groups: political entities, ethnic groupings, and religious communities.

In II Chronicles 7:14 of the Jewish scriptures we read, "If my people who are called by my name will humble themselves and pray and seek my face and turn from their wicked ways, then I will hear from heaven and will forgive their sin and heal their land." The concept of healing historical wounds has been emerging in tandem in both the spiritual and political worlds over the past twenty years. Even astute, spiritually sensitive political leaders and policy makers are recognizing that many of today's bitter and intractable conflicts are being driven in large part by unhealed collective memories. In the words of Jewish author Elie Wiesel, "That which is forgotten cannot be healed and that which is not healed becomes the cause of greater evil." When Serbian and Kosovar Albanian leaders were brought together in Rambouillet, France, in 1999 to attempt a negotiated settlement, I knew before they even sat down at the negotiating table that the efforts at third party intervention would be unsuccessful. Being personally acquainted with some of those sitting at the negotiating table, I knew better than most the extent of their captivity to bitter memories that would inhibit them from engaging in constructive problem solving. Israeli leaders liked to say of Palestinian leader, Yasser Arafat, that "he never missed a chance to miss a chance." Why is that? Because Arafat was captive to the bitter memories connected to Palestinian suffering. I am personally cautious about the possibility of any negotiated settlement between Israelis and Palestinians until there is a healing of the historical wounds of both communities. Deeply wounded communities and nations find it extraordinarily difficult to reach beyond their pain to consider the common good and engage in constructive problem solving toward a political settlement. Those who would seek to serve as third party intermediaries in some of the world's most intractable conflicts would be wise to integrate the healing of historical wounds into their strategic thinking.

In his book, *An Ethic for Enemies,* Donald Shriver points out that the twentieth century involved more violence, more human bloodshed, more refugees and displaced persons, more genocide and ethnic cleansing, and more human suffering than any century in human history. As a result, the global village is populated with wounded nations, which means that the twenty-first century promises to be the most dangerous century in all of human history. We are already seeing the tip of the iceberg in the rise of religious extremism in many faith traditions but most especially in the emergence of militant Islam. Since September 11, 2001, the operative paradigm of the international order has become security. Yet there will never be true security in a world of unhealed nations. Healing wounded nations in the twenty-first century is not an esoteric luxury but rather absolutely essential for peace in the world.

In 1989 when Slobodan Milosevic was campaigning for office in Yugoslavia, he spoke to a crowd of people in the ancient Serb heartland of Kosovo. At one point, he gestured toward Kosovo Polje and roared, "Never again!" Every Serb knew exactly what he meant. He was referring to the defeat of Prince Lazar by the Turks in 1389, which began over five hundred years of harsh Ottoman rule over Serbia. It forms part of the bitter collective memory for Serbs and, in part, explains their rationale for cleansing Europe of Muslims.

Let us now consider the impact of collective historical wounds by examining the burden of memory—which includes emotional, spiritual, and moral pain and suffering. First of all, the burden of memory mythologizes a victim/offender dynamic which creates an interdependent bondage forged of the historical pain of the victim and the historical guilt of the offender. The mythology of victimhood is often used by conquerors to mitigate their guilt and by victims to sustain their collective identity. During a service of reconciliation at Jesus Abbey in Korea in September 2000, I witnessed young Koreans wailing and lamenting with grief over the treatment of Korean women by Japanese soldiers as comfort women. Ironically, none of these young people were even alive during World War II. Yet they bore in their hearts the scars of collective humiliation and suffering at the hands of the Japanese. In a sense, they needed the Japanese to acknowledge and apologize for these actions to release them from their pain. At the same time, the Japanese needed the Koreans to forgive them and release them from their historical guilt. Such is also true in a different way in the United States, where Anglos and African Americans need each other to bring healing to a nation that still suffers from the scourge of white privilege created by the existence of slavery and historical institutional racism. Dr. Martin Luther King Jr. and other American Civil Rights leaders wisely saw that whites and blacks needed each other and would have to live together. This caused them to avoid further wounding by a strategy of reconciliation and nonviolent noncooperation. In the new South Africa that arose from the ashes of apartheid, leaders such as President Nelson Mandela and Archbishop Desmond Tutu knew that whites and blacks needed each other to rebuild that society while avoiding a racial carnage in the settling of old scores. This caused them to balance the pursuit of political and economic justice with the Truth and Reconciliation Commission so that justice would be balanced with forgiveness.   .

Second, the burden of memory creates stereotyping and demonization wherein identity-based communities hold negative images of each other. Iranian leaders at one time referred to America as the Great Satan. Americans commonly thought of Iranians as terrorists. In November 2000, I participated in a series of prayer breakfasts during an international conference in Khartoum sponsored by the International Center for Religion and Diplomacy to resolve religious issues of the war in Sudan. ICRD brought together senior-level Muslim and Christian leaders with key representatives of the international religious community. On the first morning, I sat at my appointed place and saw that I was situated next to a cleric from the Ayatollah Khomeini Theological Institute in Qom, Iran. He gave me a malevolent glance and said, "I suppose that no gathering would be complete without the imperialists." I considered a response in kind, reflecting American stereotypes of Iranians carried over from the 1979 hostage crisis at the U.S. Embassy. Instead, I acknowledged United States' disrespect for Iranians and spoke specifically about the CIA involvement in the overthrow of Prime Minister Mossadegh in 1953. I then apologized as an American and asked his forgiveness. He looked straight into my eyes for the longest time and finally said, "I suppose our taking of hostages at the embassy was wrong and, for that, I apologize." In that moment, the ice seemed to melt between us, the wall of hostility had been scaled, and created the possibility for a relationship that reached beyond our bitter history together.

Third, the burden of memory creates morally wounded worldviews in a people group where painful and traumatic historical events distort a community's sense of civility. In 1994 during a visit to Belgrade, I recall that more than one Yugoslav government official spoke of getting rid of Muslims as a necessary part of doing Europe's dirty work. They pointed out to me that none of the great powers even attempted to stop the Serbs and, in fact, quietly welcomed their efforts. During a visit to Pale in Republika Srpska, the chief advisor to President Radovan Karadzic sat and visited with us while we waited for our meeting with the prime minister. Outwardly, he looked like the headmaster of a British public school, but I remember the distinct feeling of being in the presence of evil as he smiled and paraphrased the American poet Robert Frost, "We Serbs believe that good fences make good neighbors," in response to my question about treatment of Bosnian Muslims. I remember sitting on the floor with a militant leader in a heavily guarded compound in Islamabad as he described the rationale for the armed struggle in Kashmir, knowing full well that it had contributed to an atmosphere of trauma and suffering for average Kashmiris in the Kashmir Valley. In each case, their sense of civility had been destroyed and created a worldview in which violence and suffering were not only normal but a necessary part of daily existence.

Fourth, the burden of memory is passed on to subsequent generations, and the pain and suffering is carried in their collective hearts. In 1997, I was planning to attend a meeting in Switzerland with an American Jewish leader. He asked me to make the travel arrangements for both of us. When I informed him that the best price and flight options were on Lufthansa, his immediate passionate response was, "I won't fly on that Nazi airline!" I failed to take into account the collective memory he carried in his heart as a child of Holocaust survivors whose family mostly perished in the Nazi death camps of Poland during the Second World War.

Fifth, the burden of memory involves the moral culpability of the perpetrator. How does he come to terms with the evil he has done? At the end of the Second World War, as U.S. troops swept across Germany and liberated the concentration camps, they were so appalled by what they found that they forced German citizens in the surrounding villages to go through the camps and see for themselves the results of the Final Solution. In 1994, I was invited to participate in a service of repentance at Sachsenhausen Concentration Camp near Berlin that was led by German Christian leaders and a Jewish rabbi from Jerusalem. Of the three hundred participants, the vast majority were the age of my parents, who were young adults during the war. When the opportunity was provided for participants to make a conscious act of repentance for their collaboration with the Third Reich, I was stunned by the number of Germans that streamed forward weeping and confessing aloud their oaths of loyalty to Adolf Hitler, their use of the "Sieg heil," and their inaction as Jews were rounded up by the SS. Fifty years later, they still carried the collective guilt of moral culpability in their hearts.

Finally, the burden of memory leads to a functional atheism in people groups that have suffered widespread sustained violence. In his book, *The Trial of God*, Elie Weisel shows how the theology of many Jews was simply inadequate to deal with the Holocaust. As a result, many turned to atheism, others to militancy. Among Jewish Holocaust survivors, the most prevalent question remains: "Where was God in all this?" From my extensive involvement and friendship in the Jewish community, I have observed that many Jews define Jewish identity in terms of history, culture, and tradition while at the same time professing agnosticism about God. Weisel suggests that until people relearn how to trust God, they can never trust "the other" enough to become neighbors. This same dynamic may underlie Hindu/Muslim conflicts in South Asia.

Having considered the burden of memory let us now shift our focus to the healing process. The first key element of the healing process is acknowledgment. How does a community face the truth about history? Many will say, "Why stir up old wounds?" or "Why not let sleeping dogs lie?" At a civil society forum I attended in Jammu in 2002, a professor of sociology from Mumbai University proposed what to him seemed an innovative idea of practicing intentional forgetting in Kashmir. When in 1990 Vaclav Havel was elevated from dissident playwright to president of Czechoslovakia, he publicly called on the nation to forget the past and move forward into the future. The people who supported that view most enthusiastically were the leaders of the Levy bloc, the former communists who had the most to lose by having to face the truth of history. The process of facing the truth about history is also complicated by the question of whose version of the truth should be authoritative. The same historical event has many different perspectives depending on the experience, the memory, or the retelling of the event. Here, once again, the mythology of the victim/

offender dynamic emerges as the offender seeks to mitigate guilt, and the victim clings to suffering as part of collective identity. In 1992 in the United States, we discovered that Native Americans and Anglos had very different perspectives on the founding of America in 1492 by Christopher Columbus. For Americans of European descent, it seemed to be a cause for celebration. For many people of color, it seemed to be a cause for sorrow and repentance. How do we allow the complexity of history to emerge, and how do we understand and respond to the perspective of another whose perspective differs sharply from our own? At what point does a person's perspective have to change when it is not supported by the facts? I recall on my second visit to Auschwitz that I was viewing the sobering exhibits with an Austrian friend of mine, who had been raised as a Nazi by his grandfather and father. During a time of deep spiritual conversion and renewal, he repented of his Nazi ideology. Over the past ten years, he had been working as an advocate for the Jewish community. Nevertheless, on that day I watched him shake his head in disbelief and mutter over and over again, "Lies, it was all lies. We were taught lies."

Facing the truth about history is a complex process of having an honest conversation about the past, where informed and morally courageous people determine the past hurts and injustices that must be healed. Hence, acknowledgement begins with research into the specific events, people, and places associated with historical wounds. Perhaps this can happen through truth commissions, opening official files, public trials, or documentary books and films. As communal awareness is created about the truth of historical wounds, it can foster a host of official and unofficial initiatives for healing.

The second key element of the healing process is grieving. Communities and nations that have suffered so much violence such as Kashmir, Rwanda, Uganda, Chile, or Cambodia need to deal with the bruised emotions that result from historical trauma and suffering. Collective trauma in communities can induce panic, depression, exhaustion, guilt, rage, shame, protest, anxiety, denial, numbness, fear, confusion, impaired functioning, and flashbacks in the victims. In the Kashmir Valley, where there have been some seventy thousand deaths at the hands of Indian security forces and militant groups, there are few families that have not experienced the loss of a husband, brother, son, uncle, or father. The Kashmir Valley is filled with the tears of Kashmiri suffering. Former political prisoners in Slovakia, in many ways, feel abandoned by a society that seems to care little about the trauma they suffered at the hands of the Czechoslovakian secret police during the communist rule. A great sadness still hangs like a heavy pall over Armenia almost ninety years after the 1915 genocide by the Turks. Israelis who have never really come to terms with the suffering of the Holocaust find themselves taking it out on the Palestinians in their sometimes harsh and unjust policies. Serbia is filled with hatred, which lingers just below the surface because they have never come to terms with the lingering bitterness from the Ottoman Turkish rule. In a 1987 visit to Uganda, I was staggered by the enormity of human grief and trauma that I witnessed from Idi Amin's reign of terror. Trauma therapy, a specialized process of counseling for victims of violence, is absolutely essential in these situations because, it facilitates a cleansing and healing process that allows raw emotions to surface, be expressed in a healthy, constructive manner, and create a climate of hope. Those who have never lived in societies that have been wracked by state or insurgent violence have difficulty understanding the culture of militancy and how it can take over the entire soul of the community once its sense of civility becomes distorted or destroyed.

The third element of the healing process is identificational repentance. As I discussed in chapter 7, repentance is a process of recognizing one's culpability for wrongdoing that lead's one to seek forgiveness from God and the offended party and to change one's thinking and behavior. Important questions that recovering communities need to ask themselves include, "Are we responsible only for our own actions, or do we also have a collective responsibility for the sins of our community? Are we responsible for the sins of past generations?" Can our former victims ever heal if we don't take responsibility? Can we have a future together?" Both the sacred texts and human experience would seem to suggest that there is merit in both individual and corporate responsibility. In the Jewish scriptures, we are told that the sins of the fathers and mothers are visited unto the third and fourth generation. Individual responsibility means that I am accountable to God and society for my actions as an individual. Criminal and civil law are grounded in this principle. In the collective context, I have to realize that the actions of my community or nation, which are taken on my behalf, invariably affect my relationships with other individuals, communities, and nations. Therefore, as a member of a community or nation, I must share in the collective responsibility for actions taken on my behalf even if I did not personally support or participate in those actions. In the same way, the actions of past generations of my community or nation also affect my relationships with other communities and nations. Therefore, I must share in the collective responsibility of my heritage. In 1995, I was asked to address a group of Palestinian leaders at Bethlehem Bible College. As I was introduced and then moved to the front of the room, I initially sensed and then saw the hostility toward me simply because I was an American. I quickly concluded that if I were to gain any hearing at all, I would need to acknowledge the insensitivity of the U.S. government to Palestinian suffering, which I then did so. I also spoke about my own history of friendship with key people in the Palestinian community, which seemed to thaw the ice. In South Asia, I frequently encounter considerable hostility toward the United States because of the history of CIA involvement in the region. In many ways, Kashmiri Muslims blame the United States for its role of introducing the gun culture into the region when it suited our purposes during the Soviet occupation of Afghanistan. Having been involved in many of the world's hot spots and intractable conflicts, I am only too aware of the historical wounds caused by the legacy of European colonialism.

Identificational repentance is a form of corporate confession that acknowledges the actions of one's parents, leaders, or ancestors before God and the offended party and apologizes and asks forgiveness. I first witnessed this process in 1986 in Nairobi, Kenya, when I was part of a meeting between a British and American SOMA (Sharing of Ministries Abroad) team with the Anglican archbishop of Kenya and a group of Kenyan Anglican leaders. At one point, the meeting seemed to bog down and to be going nowhere when we finally reached an impasse, and there was a long silence. Finally, one British member of the team stood up and acknowledged the painful legacy of British colonial occupation of Kenya, apologized on behalf of the British, and asked the forgiveness of the Kenyans. There was a long silence, and then the archbishop stood and spoke to the group. He acknowledged the hatred by Kenyans for all whites, as a result of the colonial occupation, and apologized and asked forgiveness to the British and Americans. Then, one American member of the team stood up and acknowledged how the United States had turned Africans into slaves in our nation, apologized, and asked forgiveness. This painful and awkward process totally transformed the environment of our whole visit. I have never forgotten that moment. This again illustrates the reciprocal nature of apology and repentance.

In 2002, during a reconciliation seminar in Gulmarg involving Kashmiri Muslims and pandits, I recall the extraordinarily tense and hostile atmosphere on the first evening. However, three days later during a service of reconciliation I witnessed senior Islamic leaders stand up, acknowledge the role of Muslims in the exodus of pandits from the valley, apologize, ask forgiveness of the pandits, and pledge to work for return of the pandits from refugee camps near Jammu to the valley. Those actions, together with others, totally transformed the atmosphere between the two communities and sent shock waves through the pandit community. I believe that on-site reconciliation ceremonies provide a context to bring together leaders and representatives of both the perpetrators and the victims for the purpose of acknowledgement, confession, apology, and forgiveness. It is important to meet on the site of the offense to bring about emotional and spiritual cleansing and healing. The ceremony should include a statement of purpose, acknowledgement of specific actions of wrongdoing by representatives of the offending party(ies), the extension of forgiveness by the offended party(ies) and a communal reconciliation meal. Such a ceremony requires careful preparation to avoid superficial confessions and responses. It should also grow out of relationship between the participants from both the offending and offended parties.

The fourth element of the healing process is restorative justice. The ancient principle of restorative justice is deeply rooted in the Abrahamic faith traditions and is based on a philosophy, in which wrongdoing is seen in terms of broken relationships rather than broken laws, and justice is the process of repairing the damage done by making amends. It is a form of justice that not only makes things right, but is also a model that affirms human dignity and respect for one another. In that sense, a situation is considered to have been made right when the offending community has acknowledged its injustice or wrongdoing, when offender and victim agree on what can be done to correct the injustice and make amends, and, finally, when the agreement is fulfilled.

The concept of restorative justice is one that not only emerges from the sacred texts but also is a century's old approach to conflict resolution practiced in more traditional societies, in tribes, and in villages. More recently, it is beginning to reemerge in Western societies in connection to the criminal justice system, and it seeks to bring victims and offenders together as an adjunct to the legal process of trial and punishment. In the Victim Offender Reconciliation Programs, victims are brought together with the perpetrators of crimes to share their perspectives on what happened, and how they are affected by it. They discuss and agree on some form of restitution to the victim. Sometimes there are apologies by the offender to the victim, and the victim has the opportunity to extend forgiveness. Having been a part of numerous such encounters, I have been struck by not only the difficulties and complexities but also seen the tremendous potential for transformation and healing in both sides.

Reconcilers should ask the question "Is it possible for restorative justice to play a role between communities torn by wrongdoing and violence?" Does it offer the same transformational potential in the healing of nations? Can representatives of offender and victim nations be brought together for an honest conversation about what happened and how their peoples were affected by it? Can they not agree on some form of restitution to the victim nation? Can there not be public apologies and forgiveness extended? In more traditional societies, this is not a novel idea because the notion of restorative justice is more deeply rooted than in the West. In Kashmir, for example, I believe it could be a very important dimension of the healing process to bring together Kashmiri leaders with Indian leaders from past and present administrations in Delhi to have an honest conversation about history leading to restitution, apologies, and forgiveness. Iran and the United States would experience a dramatic change in its relationship if such a conversation about history were held by leaders from both nations leading to restitution, apologies, and forgiveness.

Acknowledgement, grieving, repentance, and restorative justice should lead to political forgiveness as a collective act between communities. Political forgiveness is never easy. As Donald Shriver points out; it requires a courageous and generous act on the part of a community that joins memory and moral judgment with forbearance, empathy, and a commitment to a shared future with the enemy. Such is the need for our time as we enter the twenty-first century. Such is at the heart of God's great purpose in history for the healing of the nations. Such is at the heart of the Abrahamic moral vision and the key to healing the broken family of Abraham.

In conclusion, healing collective wounds is the sixth core value of faith-based reconciliation and the means to its implementation is a fourfold process of restoration of the burden of memory in a wounded community or nation.

Chapter Nine

SUBMISSION TO GOD
THE PRINCIPLE OF SOVEREIGNTY

Sovereignty is the heart of a faith-based perspective and means divine agency in human affairs in three tangible forms; supreme authority, providence and as a basis for unity.

In January 2005, I visited Damascus, Syria, to meet with Syrian officials and religious leaders to explore the possibility of a faith-based reconciliation seminar in the Middle East that would address the need for an alternative to religious extremism and also build bridges between Middle East Islamic leaders and American Christian and Jewish leaders. After hearing my message about faith-based reconciliation, Sheik Salah Kuftaro invited me to speak the next day at Abunour Mosque during Jumu'ah prayer. The next morning, as I was escorted into the mosque, I made two discoveries. First, I discovered that I would be speaking to approximately ten thousand people. Second, I discovered that there was a second speaker, the leader of one of the Islamist parties of Iraq. In my remarks, I shared with them that as children of Abraham, we shared a common challenge. At the present time, the world is being shaped by two competing ideologies grounded in a spirit of domination. One of those ideologies might be called *American primacy,* which envisions the United States as a benign hegemon in the world, imposing our will on other nations through the use of diplomatic coalitions or military force. Either way, the operative vision is remaking the world in America's image. Unfortunately, many Christians and even Jews in America tacitly and openly support this vision without realizing that it is profoundly hostile toward the Islamic world and antithetical to the Abrahamic moral vision. The second ideology might be called *global Jihad*, which is grounded in the doctrine of the sovereignty of God but understands that doctrine to mean rule by Islamic leaders and institutions. What is lacking is a pluralistic vision of how people of faith might interpret submission to God in different ways. Unfortunately, many Muslims tacitly or openly support this vision without realizing that they have embraced an understanding of the sovereignty of God that leads to a permanent state of hostility. Hence, these two moral visions are on a collision course. What is needed is the "third way" of faith-based reconciliation. This is the heart of the Abrahamic tradition and provides a common mission for the children of Abraham in the twenty-first century.

When I finished speaking and sat down, the leader of the Islamist party rose and went to the microphone. He looked visibly upset as he began his remarks. He told people that there is no "third way." There are only two ways. The way of Islam and the way of the infidel. All Muslims have a duty to conquer the infidel and extend the glory of Islam. I was sobered by his words, and yet I realized that on that January day, those people had been given two fundamental visions for the future, both grounded in the notion of the sovereignty of God: one leading to global Jihad, the other leading to the healing of the nations.

In II Chronicles 20:6 of the Jewish scriptures, we read, "Jehosophat said, 'O Lord, God of our forbears, are you not the God who is in heaven? You rule over all the Kingdom of the nations. Power and might are in your hand, and no one can withstand you.'" Elsewhere in Surah 57:2 of the Qu'ran, we read, "To him, belongs the dominion of the heavens and the earth: it is He who gives Life and Death; and He has Power over all things." In Asa page 141 in the *Guru Granth Sahib* we read, "Let compassion be your mosque, Let faith be your prayer mat, Let honest living be your Koran, Let modesty be the rules of observance, Let piety be the fasts you keep; In such wisdom try to become a Muslim: Right conduct the Ka'aba; Truth the Prophet; Good deeds your prayer; Submission to the Lord's will your rosary; Nanak, if this you do, the Lord will be your protector."

At the heart of a faith-based worldview is an orientation toward the divine: understood in some traditions as a personal God and in other traditions as the source of meaning and existence. Either way, it serves as a motivating vision for people of faith about the nature of the political order, assumptions about human nature and the purpose and goal of human history. A faith-based perspective assumes that an orientation toward the divine is a normal feature of the human mind, the normal pattern of human life, and an important foundation for healthy families, communities, and nations. A faith-based perspective assumes that spirituality, religion, and politics are inseparable. Thomas Merton, a Roman Catholic monastic and mystic wrote in his book, *The Nonviolent Alternative* in 1972, "For Gandhi, strange as it may seem to us, political action had to be by its very nature 'religious' in the sense that it had to be formed by principles of religious and philosophical wisdom. To separate religion and politics was in Gandhi's eyes 'madness' because his politics rested on a thoroughly religious interpretation of reality, of life and of men's place in the world." A faith-based perspective assumes that true reconciliation is not possible apart from the divine agency.

Jesus of Nazareth taught and modeled the principle of sovereignty. Shortly before his death, Jesus visited the Garden of Gethsemane on the Mount of Olives across from the Temple Mount in Jerusalem. There he fell on his face and prayed, "My Father, if it is possible, may this cup be taken from me. Yet not as I will, but as you will." Clearly, Jesus did not want to endure suffering and death. Yet he submitted his will to God's greater purpose. Earlier in his ministry, he arrived in the village of Bethany to visit his friends Mary, Martha, and Lazarus. Unfortunately, when Jesus arrived, he learned that their brother Lazarus had died four days earlier. He had already been buried in a tomb, and his family and friends were grieving his death. Jesus had the audacity to tell his sisters, "Your brother will rise again." Jesus then commanded that the stone entrance of the tomb be removed. He prayed a prayer of submission to God and then ordered Lazarus out of the tomb. To the utter astonishment of all, Lazarus walked out of the tomb. At the heart of Jesus's message was the concept of the kingdom or reign of God. Walter Wink wrote in his book, *When the Powers Fall: Reconciliation in the Healing of Nations*, "Jesus summed up the universal hope in the expression, 'the Kingdom of God', better translated, 'the reign of God,' since the emphasis is not on a domain so much as God's active sovereignty in the affairs of the world. The effort to heal a society racked by ethnic hatreds or exhausted by oppression can be helpfully undergirded by Jesus's message of God's reign."

The Torah teaches the principle of sovereignty. In Genesis chapter 3, God establishes the principle of divinely imposed human limits or boundaries in the Garden of Eden. In the very next chapter, the principle of divine accountability for human actions is established as Cain must answer for and experience the consequences for the murder of his brother Abel. The Book of Exodus tells the story of a nation of Hebrew slaves being released from the bitter yoke of the Egyptian pharaoh and shows a human authority being punished for steadfastly refusing to submit to God's will. The Book of Daniel tells the story of Nebuchadnezzar, the Babylonian monarch being driven to insanity and losing his kingdom for arrogantly refusing to submit to God's supreme authority. His sanity was restored only when he submitted to God.

At the very heart of the teaching of the Qu'ran is the principle of sovereignty. One might say that the very foundation of the revelation to Muhammed was the need for human submission to God. The word "Islam" means submission to God's will and assumes that this is the basis for becoming a person of faith and for the right ordering of society. More than any other faith tradition, Islam teaches us that the Abrahamic tradition centers on submission to the one true living God. Hence, the key or hinge point of faith-based reconciliation is the principle of "Islam" in its broader meaning of submission to God's authority rather than its more restricted sectarian incarnation found in historical and institutional Islam. In other words, the sacred texts show that there can be a pluralistic understanding of submission that honors and respects all people of faith who are sincerely striving to submit their lives to a divine authority and allowing that to shape their worldview.

Here is the crux of the human conundrum. There will never be peace between nations without shared submission to God's authority. At the same time, there will never be peace as long as submission is defined in narrow sectarian or institutional terms that would impose one human construct on the people of other traditions. This is at the core of the present hostility between institutional Christianity and institutional Islam. Both are animated by a missionary impulse that envisions winning over the other. For evangelical Christians, it means, "getting Muslims saved" and into a church. For Muslims committed to *dawah,* it means extending the rule of Islam or dar al-Islam into Christian territory. Evangelical Christians think of winning souls. Dawah Muslims envision ruling territory. Nevertheless, both visions are grounded in a spirit of domination and are ultimately inimical to a vision of faith-based reconciliation. Both traditions need to rediscover the ancient Abrahamic moral vision and, in doing so, will rediscover each other in a new way that will lead to the healing of the broken family of Abraham.

In the Hindu tradition, the Vedas describe Shiva as the sovereign of the gods that rules over all creatures. The Bhagavad Gita (18.66) admonishes the person of faith to abandon all supports and look to God for protection. The Hindu bhakti tradition focuses on a personal relationship with God that is achieved through surrender to God and devotional acts. The reality of submission to God was embodied most deeply in the life of Mahatma Gandhi, who found in that submission not only a deeper peace with God and self but also the basis for a pluralistic political order in South Asia. Buddhism does not teach about a personal God. Although in the Tibetan strand of Buddhism, the Buddha is looked upon by some enlightened teachers and their disciples as the incarnation of deity. Nevertheless, the dharma teaches that fear is only the beginning of faith that leads to submission to ethical precepts as the path to enlightenment. In the Sikh tradition, which seeks to be a bridge between Islam and Hinduism, the Adi Granth (Gauri M, 1 page 151) teaches that the fear of God is mighty and of great weight and that obedience to God's ordinance and will can purify the mind.

So now let us consider three facets of sovereignty: supreme authority, divine providence and also as a basis of unity. First of all, sovereignty is God's supreme authority over individuals, communities, and nations. The concept of supreme authority inspires ambivalence in the human heart. Superficially, at least, we welcome some form of supreme authority in our lives that creates structures, boundaries, and accountability. Few people truly believe that anarchy enables us to experience security and achieve our true potential as individuals and communities. Chaos and randomness undermine human relationships and societies. At the deeper level of instinct, we put self-interest above the common good and resist structures, boundaries, and accountability. The human spirit is as fragile as an eggshell, but the human drive to self-preservation and aggrandizement is like tempered steel. The desire within us to be in control of our own destiny is at the heart of our rebellion against either transcendent or temporal authority. As a person of faith, I find that acknowledging God's supreme authority over my life sets me free from the tyranny of my own selfish needs and desires. It also causes me to take a sobering look at my own behavior and that of my nation in terms of activities calculated to dominate others. As I understand the sacred texts, it is inconsistent for a person submitted to God's will to seek to exploit or dominate others. On many occasions in the course of ICRD's work of faith-based diplomacy, I have had to listen to the unflattering descriptions of U.S. policies and actions in Africa, Asia, Europe, Latin America, or the Middle East. Initially, I cannot help feeling defensive about these criticisms. I love my country, and it hurts me deeply to hear it regarded in a hostile or cynical manner. However, as a person of faith who has submitted my life to God's authority, it requires me to have a heart of humility, which means a willingness to be self-critical and open to repentance.

The word "authority" has roots in the ancient Greek word "exousia," which means the power or right to command, act, enforce obedience, or make final decisions: jurisdiction. Authority may be both ontological or conferred by some exterior source. Transcendent authority is ontological by nature in that the divine authority is a given by virtue of God's being author of the universe. Human authority, on the other hand, ultimately derives from some form of social contract.

Jesus of Nazareth spoke about supreme authority from a transcendent perspective as the Kingdom or Reign of God. The Kingdom of God is God's rule in our hearts and over our lives. God is sovereign, and we are God's subjects. It is not a political but, rather, a spiritual kingdom. The Kingdom of God is creation healed. At the heart of the Kingdom of God is the experience of reconciliation with God, self, and others. The Kingdom of God is God's new society on earth, which operates on different principles and values than the secular world. The Kingdom of God reorders and refocuses our preoccupation with materialism. It calls us to reorder our thinking with regard to social classes. It establishes a distinct moral code and a transcendent set of values, which we are invited to embrace. It is concerned with the spiritual, physical, and emotional healing of people and societies. It is able to overcome the presence and power of evil and the works of darkness. It brings about changed lives and transformed societies. Ultimately, it provides an eternal perspective to our lives.

It is human instinct to take authority into our own hands: to say, "I will be the final arbiter of my actions. I answer to no one." In light of the European renaissance, the Protestant Reformation and the Enlightenment, the concept of self-sovereignty of both the individual and the state emerged, which replaced the notion of accountability to a transcendent God with accountability to self or popular opinion as the basis of supreme authority. In the West, this has given rise to secularism that has been the basis of Western civilization for at least the last 350 years. It forms the philosophical foundation of the realpolitik approach to the affairs of nations. The logical conclusion of self-sovereignty was seen most vividly in the Judeo Christian Western world in the rise of fascism in Nazi Germany. In the Slavic world, the emergence of self-sovereignty came through the imposition of the Marxist-Leninist vision, which saw its nadir under Joseph Stalin, the greatest mass murderer in human history. In the United States, this shift has produced a nation of consumers, who have largely forgotten their responsibility as citizens.

The concept of sovereignty as supreme authority raises thorny questions of ethics in international affairs. How shall the affairs of nations be ordered—by national interest and domination or by appeal to principle? In foreign affairs, there has been a long-standing debate between two schools of thought: realism and idealism. Realism holds that the affairs of nations should be based on the national interest and the exercise of power while idealism holds that the affairs of the nations should be guided by moral principles in an ethical framework. The realist concept of raison d' état was first promulgated by Cardinal-Duc de Richelieu, of France in the seventeenth century. Raison d' état asserted that the well-being of the state justified whatever means were employed to further it. This developed into the concept of the national interest accompanied by the balance of power, which became the basis of foreign policy in the Westphalian system of nation-states, which continues today. Otto von Bismarck, prime minister of Prussia in 1862, first articulated the concept of realpolitik, asserting that relations among states are determined by raw power and that the mighty should prevail. Realpolitik married raw power and national interest. Unwittingly, Bismarck's beliefs and policies set the stage for Adolf Hitler, the Nazis, and the Third Reich.

With regard to ethical principles in the affairs of nations, more idealist figures such as Prince von Metternich, of nineteenth century Austria, believed that a shared concept of justice was a prerequisite for international order. Metternich understood justice and power to be in both a physical and moral equilibrium in the international system. In other words, an international order that is considered unjust by some of its members will be challenged sooner or later by the exercise of power. Likewise, Woodrow Wilson, who served as America's twenty-eight president (1913-1921) believed that nations should exercise the same ethical standards as individuals. In 1913, he outlined what became known as Wilsonianism, which urged an international system and diplomacy based on ethical principles. He spoke about universal law and national trustworthiness as the foundation of the international order. He believed in collective security, binding arbitration, and international institutions as a means of implementing this vision.

While Metternich and Wilson represented an ethical approach to the affairs of nations, it was Tsar Alexander I, who first suggested a faith-based perspective as the basis for the international order. He believed that the international order should be based "on the exalted truths of the eternal religion of our Savior." Having undergone a profound religious conversion, Alexander attempted to apply spiritual and ethical principles to the international system and the practice of statecraft.

Ultimately, the principle of sovereignty as God's supreme authority must take into account the complex problem of evil. Faith-based reconciliation places the locus of evil in the human soul, recognizing the potential for collective and institutional expressions of it through the state or sociopolitical movements. Such collective expressions seek to rule by terror, intimidation, or oppression. People of faith from the Abrahamic tradition understand that evil is a personal spiritual force that takes on the forms of envy, anger, hatred, and spite. Evil is a living, efficacious spiritual reality, not a mere dysfunction or byproduct of social conditions. As such, faith-based reconciliation pursues the redemption and defeat of evil as an intrinsic part of the sociopolitical healing process. This spiritual transformation is accomplished through divine intervention as demonstrated through the signs and wonders of Jesus of Nazareth in the New Testament.

Let us now consider the second facet of sovereignty, which involves divine providence or the understanding of God's intervention in the affairs of nations. Having now entered this realm, one must confess with a deep humility that it is fraught with the potential for misunderstanding, misinterpretation, and human manipulation of the sacred texts. Nevertheless, enter it we must because for the person of faith, divine agency in human affairs is at the core of a coherent worldview. It struggles with questions such as the following: where is God in world events? How do we see God's activity in the rise and fall of governments, economic systems, class struggles, political movements, and cultural revolutions? Does God have a purpose or goal to history? Does God steer only the macro events of societies and nations or only the micro events of personal decisions of individuals? Does God hold societies and nations accountable? What is the role of human free will in the decisions that shape history? What is the role of sin and evil in shaping human history? How do we distinguish between the forces of good and evil? Do all things work for God's ultimate good? How do we understand and relate to the supernatural? What is the role of prophets?

Having waded into the midst of a theological, political, and diplomatic minefield that could consume volumes of journals and books allows me to propose five key principles for navigating the complex interplay of the divine role in the affairs of nations. These principles, in part, are drawn from the insights of Douglas Hall and Rosemary Reuther in their book, *God and The Nations*. The first principle is that God's governance of the affairs of nations is indirect. One cannot deduce a simple cause and effect but rather there is a strong element of mystery. The second principle is that God's governance is implemented in ways that leave intact human free will. The third principle is that God's governance is meant to inspire hope rather than certitude. The fourth principle is that God's governance involves the work of individual and collective transformation. The fifth principle is that God's governance has healing and restoration as it's ultimate goal: the healing of people, families, communities, and nations.

For people of faith, it is the discipline of prayer and fasting that translates the principle of sovereignty into practice. Prayer and fasting, more than any other spiritual discipline, assumes God's intervention in human affairs and treats it not as something that is subject to manipulation or appeasement of the divine but rather as an expression of human dependence and trust in a loving and compassionate God. The motto "In God we trust" that is chiseled into the stone or wood of the chambers of the U.S. Congress and is imprinted on all U.S. currency is more than a hollow and empty statement. It is a ringing declaration that affirms that the health of nations is an outgrowth of God's sovereignty. During the darkest days of the American Civil War, President Abraham Lincoln issued a proclamation declaring a national day of prayer and fasting in hope of God's intervention in a tragic fratricidal war. In ICRD's first major project in Sudan, which involved bringing senior-level Muslim and Christian leaders together to address religious issues in the conflict, we utilized a prayer and fasting team. The team met all day during the proceedings in a room adjacent to the deliberations. I shuttled back and forth each day to bring the latest update on the deliberations so as to inform the prayers of our team.

Finally, let us consider the third facet of sovereignty, which is its role as the basis for unity. There is something within our human makeup that causes us to yearn for a universal synthesis. Is there a person, a principle, a religion, an institution, or organization that can unite all the diverse peoples of the earth? We should approach this subject by examining first the nature of unity.

In the social sphere, unity is characterized by harmony, diversity, and community. Harmony assumes that there is a common collective identity, a consensus around a common set of core values, peaceful resolution of conflicts, the potential for forgiveness in relationships, a just society based on the common good, and a respect for each person and their property. Whenever one of these qualities is absent, there will generally be a state of disharmony and potential civil violence. In the aftermath of the May 1992 riots in Los Angeles, it was discovered that the flash point leading to violence was not the verdict in the Rodney King trial but rather the tensions between African American residents and Korean business owners. A clash in cultures caused blacks to feel disrespected by Koreans, and the anger and frustration level finally boiled over into civil violence. Nevertheless, three hundred years of simmering black rage formed a basic underlying cause of communal disharmony. In 1979 in Iran, the long-standing frustration with the repressive rule of the Shah and the lack of respect by America toward Iran, as an ancient and proud nation with a positive role to play as a regional power, catalyzed in a religious revolution inspired by the charismatic leadership and the teachings of Ayatollah Khomeini. America became the "Great Satan." U.S. hostages were taken for 479 days, which escalated the communal disharmony between the West and the Islamic world.

Diversity pertains to a community or nation-state, which is made up of persons or groups, which differ in ancestry, tribe, race, language, culture or political ideology. Not only are there distinctions, but the various groups in the community are aware of them which creates a potential "us vs. them" dynamic. In chapter 2, I began by saying that in many respects both domestic and international politics of the twenty-first century have become the politics of identity, which implies that cross-cultural differences will serve as a primary factor in conflict. Many leaders and policy makers fail to wrestle deeply with the complexity of how diversity can be translated into unity. It is one thing to celebrate diversity. It is quite another to engage in the difficult and painful task of creating unity in the midst of diversity. And yet that is one of the most important tasks of the twenty-first-century leader. So how do political, religious, and community leaders play a role in establishing common ground? First, they must recognize and accept that diversity is a gift of God that is not meant to be diminished, and yet it is not meant to be an end in and of itself. Secondly, they should not assume that diversity can be translated into unity by merely seeking the lowest common denominator. Few identity-based groups are willing to subordinate their own interests unless the common good takes into account their deeply held core values, even if they are able to articulate them only vaguely. Thirdly, community or national leaders will need to be intentional in bringing identity-based group leaders together to build relationship and to establish common ground. In general, it will not happen on its own. It requires visionary and proactive leadership. Finally, identity-based groups need to be encouraged to examine their own symbols, teachings, mythology, history, aspirations, and fears—both to understand more fully who they are and to see how these create or contribute to hostility toward other groups.

The third element of unity is community. This assumes that the members of different identity-based groups are willing to interact with those who are different than themselves. The concept of community assumes the existence of an implied or stated social contract in which there exists the commitment to seek the common good. Without an implied or stated social contract to seek the common good, there is no community, only interest groups pressing their own narrow agendas of group privilege. Community assumes that there must be an intentional process of building bridges so as to forge a oneness in the heart or soul of the community. Identity-based groups can live side by side with each other in a spirit of tolerance and coexistence, but let us not assume for one moment that this represents true unity.

The search for unity is painful and revealing about our own hearts because it requires an honest look at ourselves, our relationships, our prejudices, and our value systems. The search for unity may challenge our passion for received truth. Although revealed truth is absolute in nature, human experience is such that each of us apprehends truth through the grid of our own experience, and it must be balanced with our commitment to seek unity with those who view truth very differently than ourselves. How is it possible to do that, to balance our conviction about truth with a commitment to unity? At one end of the spectrum is the person or group who is so committed to the truth that it must come at the expense of living cooperatively with "the other" and seeking the common good. At the other end of the spectrum is the person or group that is so passionate for unity that it comes at the cost of having no real settled convictions. Most individuals and groups find themselves living somewhere in the tension between truth and unity. However, allow me to sound a warning to those who are passionately committed to truth at the expense of unity. You are, perhaps without realizing it, advocating uniformity, not unity; and you may actually find yourself opposing God's greater purpose in the world, which is unity. Allow me also to sound a warning to those who are passionately committed to unity at the expense of truth. Bear in mind that the sacred texts all assume that there is a divine moral grain to the universe, which means that there are moral absolutes. Unity that is based on the lowest common denominator that offends no one and affirms no truth is not unity. True unity is based on transcendent truth, which no one person or group fully apprehends. As the apostle Paul wrote in the New Testament, "We see through a glass darkly." Humility demands that we keep this perspective.

So what is the path to unity? At the most rudimentary level is a survival-based unity based on simple common interests such as a common enemy or family bonds. However, the increasingly interdependent and globalized world of the twenty-first century points to the need for a deeper and more inclusive basis for unity. The path to unity is further complicated by the profoundly different worldviews of people of faith and secular people. For people of faith, any attempt to forge common ground that is not based on a fundamental orientation toward the divine is inherently incomplete. At the same time, for secular people such as humanists and agnostics, attempts to impose a religious worldview as a basis for the common good is fraught with historical and contemporary baggage packed to overflowing with intolerance, oppression, violence, suffering, and genocide in the name of God. Even among people of faith, there is little common ground between adherents to the Abrahamic tradition and those following the Indian indigenous religious traditions such as Hinduism and Buddhism. Even among the cousins of the Abrahamic tradition—Jews, Christians, and Muslims—there is a long history of hostility, misunderstanding, demonization, and attempts to dominate the other. Nevertheless, the path to unity is not an all-or-nothing endeavor but rather a gradational experience that ranges from the basic humanitarian bonds that are cemented by a set of shared core values to the intimate fraternal bond shared by people of faith that is oriented toward the divine. The first is a principle-based unity, and the second is a sovereignty-based unity.

A principle-based unity is when common identity is built around a set of communal principles or core values. In 1989, President Wee Kim of Singapore, in his address opening the parliament, spoke about the need to identify the core values, which were held in common by Singapore's various ethnic and religious communities. Extensive public discussion led to five core values, which were seen as capturing the essence of being Singaporean: nation before ethnic group and society above self; the family as a basic unit of society; regard and community support for the individual; consensus instead of contention; and racial and religious harmony.

Might I suggest as a basis of principle-based unity the framework of civic reconciliation, which embodies eight core values:

- The pluralistic nature of creation: gender, ethnicity, race, and culture—which means that we seek unity in the midst of diversity.
- Compassionate inclusion of all people in a society based on unconditional love, which includes embrace of one's enemies.
- Peaceful resolution of conflict between individuals and groups.
- Social justice as the basis for right ordering of relationships and structures in the society.
- Forgiveness as a bedrock principle both in relationships between individuals and between communities and nations.
- The healing of historical wounds that stem from exclusion, prejudice, conflict, injustice, or unforgiveness that hold back a community's true potential for growth and development.
- Sovereignty embodied in submission to an ethical worldview, leaders guided by moral principles, religious freedom, individual and collective accountability, and a prophetic voice and moral conscience in society.
- Atonement embodied in a respect for spiritual hunger and the search for the divine or with one's own being.

I believe that this framework of civic reconciliation is one that truly captures the common good for any society as well as forming the basis or paradigm for shaping the international order of the twenty-first century. Nevertheless, as a person of faith, I must confess that I find it not completely adequate because it fails to take into account that approximately 85 percent of the world's population are people of faith, who believe in a personal God or in some form of higher power. It also fails to take into account that over three billion people are part of the family of Abraham: Jews, Christians, and Muslims—who hold as the very center of their being the reality and experience of submission to the one true God. In other words, unity for the family of Abraham is sovereignty based. Whether in the Torah, the New Testament, or the Qu'ran, this sovereignty-based unity is described in a spiritual entity known as the Kingdom or Reign of God, spoken about earlier in this chapter. Abrahamic peoples understand the

Kingdom of God as universal and inclusive. All are welcome regardless of race, gender, ethnicity, social class, or political ideology. In other words, nation—whether political, ethnic, or religious—is not the basis of unity. However, people of faith also recognize the Kingdom of God as intimate and personal. Each of us must make a personal decision of submission. Hence, the benefits of the Kingdom of God are available to all people but must be personally appropriated by each of us. People of the Abrahamic tradition truly believe that the Kingdom of God makes a unique offer: the possibility of true reconciliation that is appropriated by faith.

I would like to conclude this chapter by considering the unique role of Jesus of Nazareth in the quest for unity. In doing so, one must acknowledge the pivotal role and honor the prophetic figures that have shaped our understanding of faith-based reconciliation as a reflection of the heartbeat of the one true living God. I acknowledge and honor Moses who was the recipient of the five books of the Torah, which were meant to be more than the basis of a private relationship with God. It was the core of a moral vision for society intended to form the basis of cultural values, institutions, and presuppositions in the society that became known as Israel. In that sense, I give thanks for my Jewish cousins and the gift of Torah to all of us. I acknowledge and honor Gautama Buddha, who gave to us the Noble Eightfold Path as a practical guide to enlightenment. It reminds us that faith-based reconciliation is a journey of the soul, a spirituality that involves intense inner struggle as well as social engagement. I give thanks for my Buddhist and Hindu friends and the gift of dharma to all of us. I acknowledge and honor Muhammed, who was the recipient of the Qu'ran and who, more than any other prophetic figure, recalled us to the original Abrahamic vision that faith is embodied in submission to the one true living God. I give thanks for my Muslim cousins and the gift of Islam to all of us. At the same time, I must assert that Jesus plays a unique role in all of human history in that healing and reconciliation were at the heart of his personhood, message, and activities. Reconciliation was, in a sense, his unique legacy to the human race. Dr. Martin Luther King Jr. wrote in 1967, "Jesus is eternally right. History is replete with the bleached bones of nations that refused to listen to him." Perhaps if we can uncouple Jesus of Nazareth from historical, ideological, and institutional Christianity, we can approach him afresh as someone who has something to say to our time and to our situation in the twenty-first century. Mahatma Gandhi, although a devout Hindu, was drawn to the life and teachings of Jesus of Nazareth. In the living quarters of his ashram, he had only one picture on the wall, an artist's rendering of Jesus. Those who were closest to Gandhi knew that he had a great love for Jesus and attempted to model his life and work on the Sermon on the Mount.

So who was and is Jesus of Nazareth? Jesus is perhaps one of the most famous figures in human history. However, even two thousand years after his appearing on the stage of history, he remains an enigma and a challenge for many. The New Testament affirms that Jesus was Jewish, a son of the commandment. He was born to Joseph of Nazareth and Mary yet conceived by the Spirit of God. His ministry comprised three years almost entirely in Israel. His message focused on the Kingdom or Reign of God. He called twelve disciples or followers around him and shaped and molded them. He performed signs and wonders as a supernatural expression of the presence of God's reign in our midst. He came specifically to Israel but envisioned the Abrahamic blessing of reconciliation for all nations. He embodied the Abrahamic tradition in submitting his life to God's will and taught others to do likewise. He was betrayed by one of his own disciples and put to death on a cross by the Jewish and Roman authorities not for anything he did but for who he claimed to be. He was buried in the tomb of Joseph of Arimathea, and, on the third day, his followers found the tomb was empty. These are the basic assertions of the New Testament about the life of Jesus. However, the Jewish prophets cause us to look at Jesus through a broader lens of history and God's purposes first embodied in Abraham, the person of faith.

The prophet Isaiah revealed in 52:13-53:12 the divine promise that, one day, God would send a messianic healer and reconciler. This messianic reconciler would universalize the Abrahamic tradition of *tikkun olam* for all the nations. In the New Testament, book of Acts (8:35), we are told about a Ethiopian government official traveling in the Gaza Strip in his chariot, and he was reading this very passage of Isaiah. At one point, he encountered a man named Philip, showed him the passage, and asked, "Of whom does the prophet speak?" It was at that moment that Philip revealed that Jesus of Nazareth was that long-awaited messianic reconciler. This poses two fundamental questions. Was and is Jesus of Nazareth God's chosen instrument for the healing of the nations? If so, how do you maintain the integrity of your own faith tradition and embrace Jesus as a healer and reconciler?

For our Abrahamic cousins from the Muslim tradition, I should remind you that the Qu'ran speaks prominently of Jesus and that he should be honored as one of the long line of prophets. What does it mean to honor him? To begin with, it means learning about the person and teachings of Jesus from the primary source, the New Testament. It has been my experience through much of the Islamic world that while many Muslims speak of Jesus as one of their prophets and as honoring him, that in reality they know very little about him from original source documents. Secondly, to honor him as well as other prophetic figures, including Muhammed, it means becoming committed to faith-based reconciliation as a prophetic movement. As one Islamic scholar in Kashmir pointed out to me, "Every prophetic movement in history has had at its heart the message of faith-based reconciliation."

For Abrahamic children from the Jewish tradition, the person of Jesus presents a unique challenge. Clearly, Jesus was Jewish, and yet he is profoundly estranged from his own people, not because of anything that he did but for what his followers have done to the Jewish people over the past two thousand years. The long history of Christian anti-Semitism is shameful and leaves Christians with very little moral high ground. From the patristic fathers to present-day hostility toward Israel and the Jewish people, Christians are an embarrassment to Jesus and a significant stumbling block to the realization of the Abrahamic vision of blessing for all the nations. Nevertheless, in the same way that Joseph needed to be reconciled to his own brothers in Genesis 45:1-15, too, will Jesus need to be reconciled to his own people, Israel. It is an essential part of the healing process that will release the Abrahamic blessing. This does not mean conversion to Christianity. Jews and Muslims need to find a way to be faithful to their own traditions while embracing Jesus as a healer and reconciler.

In conclusion, sovereignty is the seventh core value of faith-based reconciliation, and it means supreme authority, divine providence, and the basis for unity. Sovereignty is at the heart of a faith-based worldview.

Chapter Ten

FINDING PEACE WITH GOD
THE PRINCIPLE OF ATONEMENT

Atonement means that, ultimately reconciliation is the process of finding peace with God.

One of the practices of faith-based diplomacy that I spoke about in chapter 5 is the spiritual conversation. One evening in spring 1996, my colleague Juraj Kohutiar from Slovakia and I were taken to dinner by a Serbian cabinet minister at a restaurant in Belgrade. During the course of the meal, I took a risk and raised the question of this senior government official's relationship with God. This began a two-hour conversation, wherein he described his spiritual struggles and his search for God. He shared with us that he had been raised on Marxist dogma since childhood but that it still left his soul empty. He asked for our wise counsel, which provided the opportunity for us to honor the spiritual hunger in his heart and to challenge him to think about faith-based reconciliation, not only in its application to the sociopolitical situation in Yugoslavia but also to his own search for God.

Thomas Merton, a Roman Catholic monastic and mystic, wrote, "To reconcile man with man and not with God is to reconcile no one at all." This points to a fundamental truth often overlooked: that to be human is to be on a spiritual quest or journey toward a deeper understanding of the purpose of life. Is there a God? What is God's nature? Is it possible to have a relationship with God? Does my life have meaning and purpose? Who am I? Where do I come from? Where am I going? This journey and the questions that accompany it are all part of that process of finding peace with God. The sacred texts call this process atonement.

Jesus of Nazareth taught the principle of atonement. On one occasion, a rich young man ran up to him and asked, "What must I do to inherit eternal life?" Jesus responded by reminding him of some of the commandments in the Torah at which the young man brightened up and indicated that he had observed all these laws since he was a youth. Jesus then told him, "You lack one thing. Go sell all your have and give it to the poor, and you will have treasure in heaven. Then, come, follow me." Throughout his public ministry, Jesus was inviting people to take the step of faith by surrendering their hearts to God and making God the center of their lives. In essence, he offered them the gift of eternal life, which could only be appropriated by faith. The Torah teaches the principle of atonement. In Genesis chapter 3, God creates human beings to be in a relationship with him. At the same time, the reality of sin enters the pictures as a barrier to relationship with God. Adam and Eve, as the prototypical human beings, are created not only to be in a relationship with each other but also in relationship with God. However, one of the conditions of that relationship is living within divinely imposed boundaries symbolized by God's restricting the couple from eating from the tree of knowledge of good and evil. Later, when they willfully choose to violate those boundaries, they experienced the consequences: alienation from God in the form of banishment from the Garden of Eden and estrangement from each other in the form of relationships built on domination and suffering. However, the Book of Leviticus tells us that God makes provision to overcome that estrangement through the Day of Atonement also known as Yom Kippur. The Qu'ran teaches the principle of atonement. In Surah 2:160-162, it says that repentance, making amends and openly declaring the truth, is the key to God's mercy and blessing. It sternly warns that those who reject faith and die rejecting on them is God's curse. The Qu'ran teaches that the heart of faith is in the act of surrender or submission to the will of God, a concept which we will explore later in this chapter. The Hindu tradition teaches the principle of atonement. The Mundaka Upanishad teaches that all evil effects of human deeds are destroyed when he who is personal and impersonal is realized (Mundaka Upanishad 2.2.9). The Bhagavad Gita teaches that he who turns to God in love and utter devotion will have the sins of a lifetime removed (Bhagavad Gita 9:30-3). The Buddhist tradition teaches the principle of atonement. In "Meditation on Buddha Amitayus 3.30," there is an admonition to contemplate the Buddha and utter his name ten times to expiate sin. Nirvana is the ultimate aim of Buddhists, which is achieved in this life and not gained after death. The Sikh tradition teaches the principle of atonement. The Adi Granth (Sri Ragu MS page 70) teaches that contemplation of Naam (the name of God) can save a person from the five cardinal vices. It also teaches that there is no peace with God without meditation on God's name.

In this chapter, we will consider four facets of atonement: spiritual hunger, estrangement, faith, and transformation. First, let us consider the element of spiritual hunger. The sacred texts teach us that our human nature is made up of three constituent elements: body, soul, and spirit. The body (sarx) is that part of our being that interacts with the physical and social environment: sight, sound, smell, taste, touch, talk, walk, and feel. The soul (psyche) is that part of our being that consists of our intellect, our emotions, and our volition or will. The spirit (pneuma) is that part of our being that is meant to connect and be nurtured by a relationship with the divine. It is nourished by the metaphysical and supernatural dimensions of reality that transcend logic and rationality. It is a world of angels, demons, miracles, visions, healings, and prophecies. It is a world of spiritual power, light, and darkness that is invisible to the naked eye, and yet it shapes much of what is ultimately experienced in the physical world. It is a world of prayer, praise, prophecy, and ecstatic utterance that gives voice to the soul's deepest yearnings toward the creator of the universe. The sacred texts also teaches us that the human spirit, to be properly functioning, must be connected to the spirit of God, and to receive continual divine nourishment that then guides our intellect, emotions, will, and body. When the human spirit is lacking this connection to the divine, it is like an unused muscle that atrophies. To compensate for a shriveled spirit, the soul takes control—which means that the person is guided primarily by their intellect (what makes sense), their emotions (what feels right and good), or their volition (what is desired). An atrophied spirit leading to a controlling soul is the very condition of spiritual hunger.

Just as our body provides certain signs indicative of physical deprivation such as hunger pains, thirst, or breathlessness, so our soul and spirit provide telltale signs of spiritual deprivation. Some of these symptoms include a sense of something missing in one's life, a feeling that one's life has no meaning or purpose, a sense of prolonged inner emptiness, a sense of guilt, or a feeling that life is about survival. Spiritual hunger is a cry from deep within us to be in relationship with the living God, to have meaning and purpose in our life, and to be free of guilt, burden, and emptiness. The symptoms of spiritual hunger can be ignored for years or even a whole lifetime, but they never completely disappear.

Since spiritual hunger is a universal human condition, one might be tempted to probe its origin. To do this, we need to consider the nature of estrangement or alienation. It was Karl Marx, in fact, who popularized the word "alienation," having taken it from the German theologian, Ludwig Feuerbach. Marx applied this concept to his dialectical analysis and understood the plight of the proletariat in terms of economic alienation. In the 1960s, the term became more political than economic as tens of thousands of Americans and Europeans took to the streets and campuses a sense of alienation and frustration with politics as usual. However, the sacred texts speak about a much more fundamental alienation, which is at the core or essence of the human predicament, the experience of alienation from God, which has two elements: estrangement and exclusion. The theological word for this state of being is "sin," a word which means "missing the mark" because of self-assertion and rebellion against God. Sin brings about estrangement because it acts as a barrier between us and a holy, loving God. It creates a sense of hostility between God and the person. It obstructs God's purpose in our lives. It causes damage in our relationship with others. Sin brings about exclusion since the sacred texts all make it clear that it removes us from God's presence, both in the present and, potentially, for all eternity. Sin is serious and must be confronted. There is no ignoring reality. A barrier remains a barrier until it is removed. Hence, God's answer to spiritual hunger and alienation is atonement, which is the process of becoming a person of faith.

I grew up as a religious person—who attended worship services on a regular basis, who was active in a local church, and who believed the sacred texts and the creeds of the church. Nevertheless, until the age of twenty-two, I lacked an intimate relationship with God. I could not honestly claim that I had submitted my will to God's will. This state of affairs manifested itself in my life by various expressions of spiritual hunger. As hard as I tried, nothing—politics, scholarship, or romance—could satisfy that deep yearning of my own spirit to be in a relationship with the living God.

What does it mean to be a person of faith? How does one become a person of faith and find peace with God? From the perspective of the Abrahamic tradition, Moses, Jesus, and Muhammed all pointed back to Abraham as the prototypical person of faith. From a background steeped in polytheism, Abraham became the first person in recorded history to become a monotheist, a follower of the one true living God. His journey, which becomes the paradigm for becoming a person of faith, involved four basic elements: acknowledgement, repentance, submission, and confession.

Acknowledgement is a complex process wherein a person becomes aware of their own sense of estrangement and need for God. The journey of acknowledgement might be a relatively short one or might comprise years of searching. Nevertheless, the awareness of the need for God is not a yearning for dogma; it is a cry for relationship. Acknowledgement also involves having to face the truth about ourselves, that we possess no intrinsic righteousness in the presence of a holy God. All of our illusions that we are a good person or morally superior to others or that we can control our destiny come crashing down, as they must. Once our illusions about ourself and our control over our destiny have been shattered, our heart is ready for repentance.

The concept of repentance is at the heart of becoming a person of faith, particularly in the Abrahamic tradition. Repentance begins with the recognition of shame and disgrace. There has been behavior, which has expressed disloyalty and dishonor to God. Repentance leads to a changed heart, which results in changed thinking and, ultimately, changed behavior. We come before the one true God with nothing to offer. We come before the creator of the universe with our hands outstretched like a beggar. We come before the throne of the king not to negotiate as an equal but to joyfully receive grace and mercy. We no longer have any illusions about ourself or the world in which we live. Suddenly, our eyes are opened, and we begin to see our world through God's perspective. However, repentance will only be a fleeting encounter with the divine if it is not coupled with submission.

Submission to God begins with a conscious act of surrender. It means acknowledging to God and yourself that you are giving up control of your life and accepting God's will and plan for your life. It means allying yourself with God's great purpose in history and discovering your part in it. It means that the most important question in making critical decisions is "What is God's will? How can I honor God and bring glory to him?" It means giving up any goal of dominating others or imposing our will on others. In essence, it means dying to self so that we can live for one supreme purpose: to bring honor and glory to God. However, submission to God will soon become visible to others and, hence, the need for confession.

Many years ago, I learned that when a person became a member of the Communist party that their first activity was to be assigned to selling copies of the party newspaper on the streets. In a sense, it was an act of confession, of publicly declaring one's new allegiance. Such is also true in becoming a person of faith. In the Jewish tradition, there is the Shma, "Hear O Israel, the Lord our God is one." In the Christian tradition, there is the baptismal declaration, "Jesus is Lord!" In the Islamic tradition, there is the Shahada, "There is no God but Allah, and Muhammed is his prophet!" Each of these is a form of confession, wherein the person of faith publicly declares his new allegiance. In essence, for a person of faith, their highest loyalty is no longer to family, clan, or nation but to God. Hence, ruthless dictators such as Josef Stalin inherently feared people of faith because he knew that their highest loyalty was not to the state but to God.

Atonement finds its historical roots in the biblical provision of Yom Kippur. For the Jewish people, the most solemn day of the year is Yom Kippur, the Day of Atonement. The focus of the Day of Atonement was on putting away both individual sin as well as the collective sins of the nation. It consisted of two key ceremonies: the entry of the high priest into the holy of holies in the temple and the placing of the sins of the people on the scapegoat. The entry into the holy of holies had to do with gaining access to God: coming into God's presence. The placing of the sins of the nation on the scapegoat had to do with forgiveness. In the Christian tradition, the most solemn period of the year is Holy Week and Easter. It traces the footsteps of Jesus to the cross, his death, and, three days later, his resurrection. The cross is understood by followers of Jesus as the supreme act of atonement in human history. God is offering reconciliation to each of us through the sacrifice of Jesus on the cross. In the Islamic tradition, the discipline of the five pillars—confession, prayer, fasting, almsgiving, and pilgrimage—are outward expressions that a person has embraced atonement through Islam and become a person of faith.

Acknowledgement, repentance, submission, and confession are the common threads of becoming a person of faith. Nevertheless, the true test of being a person of faith is the experience of transformation, of God continually changing the heart and life of the person. The first thing that often changes is the person's worldview. Their eyes are opened; and they see the events of their life, their community, and the nations from a transcendent perspective. They see both God and the powers of darkness at work in the world in a startlingly clear perspective. Another change is the person's desires. They find themselves turning to prayer and the sacred texts. They begin to enter into corporate worship. They desire association with other people of faith. Another change has to do with the person's focus changing from self-interest to concern for common good. Instead of asking, "What's in it for me? How will this advance my interests?' The person will ask, "What is the common good? What is just? What is right?" Another change has to do with the person's past. They may find themselves asking people for forgiveness or making amends. They may find themselves confronting unforgiveness in their own heart and having to let go of it. Another change is the person's ethical behavior. They will find themselves wanting to shape their life around the moral laws of the universe. It will affect their treatment of people and their private and public conduct. Another change is the person making peace with enemies. The sacred texts teach us that you cannot claim to love God and hate your brother or sister. Another change has to do with the person's future, giving up their own hopes and dreams, and allowing God to shape their path. They will see God utilize all their gifts, skills, and experiences and shape them into a creative future that is not only more exciting but leaves one feeling at the end of the day that peace that defies human understanding.

In conclusion, atonement is the eighth core value of faith-based reconciliation. Atonement is a process of acknowledgement, repentance, submission, and confession—which leads to transformation of the person.

Chapter Eleven

AN AGENDA FOR THE TWENTY-FIRST CENTURY

In spring 1982, I was on a spiritual retreat in the San Diego area with my friend and mentor, Father Francis Maguire. Frank, one of the earliest pioneers of the charismatic renewal in the Anglican Communion, was originally from Belfast, Northern Ireland. Even though he had made his home in the United States, he still maintained his ties with Northern Ireland through regular visits to family and friends. Following the death of the Maze Prison hunger strikers, Frank read an interview in the newspaper written about a Catholic priest, Father Brian MacRaios, whose brother, Raymond, had been one of the deceased hunger strikers. Frank was deeply moved by the transparent pain that was revealed in the article, so much so, that he felt moved to write a letter to Father MacRaios with a deeply reconciling spirit, Protestant to Catholic. This began a correspondence and visits leading to a deep friendship between the two men. As Frank shared with me this initial experience of "chancing the arm," he had no way of knowing that he was planting an initial seed in my heart. In many ways, this book and my passion for the message of faith-based reconciliation are a tribute to Frank Maguire. His friendship and exhortation have kept me going in times of discouragement or lack of direction.

In July 1984, my family and I made our way to Pretoria, South Africa, where we spent three months on sabbatical. I had been invited by Africa Enterprise of South Africa and the Anglican Diocese of Pretoria to do some teaching and training of clergy and lay leadership in the South African churches. However, while I was there, I encountered people like Stephen Hayes, Dawn Leggat, Richard Kraft, John Tooke, Michael Cassidy, Prince James Mahlangu, Ben Photolo, and others, who were people of deep faith and who were also courageously working for reconciliation in South Africa. What I didn't fully realize at the time was that through them, God was cultivating that seed in my heart that would bear fruit years later. In many ways, this book and my passion for the message of faith-based reconciliation are a tribute to them. On September 11, 2001, I received e-mails expressing concern and compassion from friends all over the world; but the one from Dawn Leggat ended with this prophetic exhortation, "I feel, beloved friend, that you were born for such a time as this."

In March 1990, during my first visit to east Central Europe, my companions and I were meeting with Dr. Geza Nemeth, a Reformed Church pastor who had a ministry of compassion that consisted of caring for Hungarian refugees from Transylvania. I wish that I could tell you that the two-hour meeting had been an unqualified success. However, it was a disaster. A test of wills emerged between one of the members of my team and Pastor Nemeth, which seemed to take us far afield from the original purpose of our meeting. Later, as the three of us sat in a Budapest café, I found myself despondently wondering how God might redeem such a disastrous meeting. One of the team members recalled Pastor Nemeth's request of us to visit his son, Geza Jr. We had promised that we would do so. Several days later, when we returned to Budapest from Bucharest, Romania, we contacted Geza Jr. and went over to his home. During the course of our visit, Geza Sr. arrived and sat quietly, listening to the conversation. Finally, he spoke up and said, "Today, unlike our last meeting, I feel that I have heard your hearts, and I would like to share with you a vision that I have never shared with anyone else, including members of my own family. I have carried in my heart for many years the dream of reconciliation beginning here in the heart of Europe and spreading, in the fullness of God's time, to nations and peoples around the globe." As he shared his vision of faith-based reconciliation, something stirred deep within my own heart. Somehow, I knew that day, at the age of forty, I was hearing the call to my life's work—becoming an instrument of reconciliation. In many ways, this book and my passion for the message of faith-based reconciliation are a tribute to Geza Nemeth. He never lived to see that dream come about; but he planted a seed in my heart that I have since carried to Africa, Asia, Europe, and the Middle East.

In chapter 1, I stated that as we enter the twenty-first century, it is the fullness of time for us to revisit the Abrahamic tradition and mission as a sweeping transcendent moral vision that, if implemented in the form of faith-based reconciliation, promises to be a spiritual, social, political, and economic revolution in the affairs of nations. The Abrahamic tradition is an ancient but radical moral vision, which points us toward the very heart of the divine and the purpose of human history: the healing of nations. The twentieth century was, without question, the most violent century in human history. Hence, the twenty-first century is the fullness of time for healing and restoration. This suggests a full agenda for those who would answer the call to be agents of reconciliation.

One item on the agenda is the casting of vision, which takes one of two forms. First, it involves empowering estranged or conflicted parties or communities to embrace a new reality and a new relationship with each other. Each of the major religions contains an ethic of moral absolutes, which govern human relationships and structures. Sometimes an appeal to those very principles creates an emotional and spiritual dynamic that enables parties in conflict to move toward reconciliation. Second, casting vision means the development of reconciliation as an ongoing moral vision for a particular society regardless of whether or not it is embroiled in a conflict so that it becomes a permanent center of gravity in that society.

The casting of vision must be seen as a long-term strategic process that requires focus, courage, patience, and the willingness to suffer. However, people of faith also understand that the function of leadership is not to cast our own personal vision but rather to be prophetic in nature by pointing people toward the transcendent vision of faith-based reconciliation, which has been unfolding throughout human history and yet has not been fully realized.

The casting of vision begins with a seed planted in the ground in the form of articulating the basic concept of reconciliation over and over again until it begins to penetrate the hearts of people in your community or sphere of influence. Rarely, if ever, do people grasp a profound moral vision the first time that it is articulated. Hence, you will need to make the word "reconciliation" part of your standard vocabulary and focus. You will need to speak about and write about it over and over again until it begins to take hold in the life of your community. In essence, imparters of vision empower a community to rise above the status quo and embrace a new reality.

How do you know that the community is grasping the vision of faith-based reconciliation? First of all, it will stimulate a communal conversation. It will stimulate debate in the public realm of newspapers, television, and literature. It will enter into conversation in families, civil society forums, and other networks of social interaction. There will be proponents and opponents. People will begin to wrestle with the difficult questions posed by the vision of faith-based reconciliation. What does it mean for our society, for my family, and for me? Does reconciliation mean cheap compromise by sacrificing my deeply held core values? Is pluralism intrinsically good? Why should I waste my valuable time building bridges to "the other?" Do I really have hostility and prejudice in my heart, or is it simply good judgment? What does an inclusive community look like? How can one be inclusive of things that are irreconcilable? Is it really possible to live in a nation or an international community, where there is peaceful resolution of conflicts? Do I believe in just war, or am I a pacifist? Is it possible to achieve a truly just society that is based on the common good and the sharing of privilege? Can one achieve true justice simply by changing systems and structures? Does forgiveness toward the offender mean giving up the pursuit of justice? How do I forgive the unforgivable? What are the greatest wounds in my nation's history? How do we go about healing those historical wounds that hold back our communal potential? What does it mean to be a nation under God? How can our leaders be encouraged to govern with spiritual and moral principles? Am I at peace with God? What is the path to peace with God? How do I become a person of faith? As these and other related questions begin to surface in the public and private discourse, you will know that you have stimulated a communal conversation.

Secondly, you will know that a community is grasping the vision of reconciliation when you begin to see transformed hearts and behaviors in the people. They will begin to draw upon the lexicon of reconciliation to analyze their own lives and situations. Some will become intentional bridge builders by reaching out to "the other" and quietly building relationships. Some will work at bringing people together for dialogue to create relationships across barriers of hostility. Enemies will be reaching out to each other to make peace. Some will feel drawn to conflict resolution, functioning as mediators and arbitrators in different situations. Some will become passionate advocates for social justice. Apologies and forgiveness will become an expected and normal activity as a response to broken relationships. People will begin to work on long-term estranged relationships. Some will begin researching the historical wounds of communities or nations and drawing the victims and offenders together in ceremonies of reconciliation. Some will work quietly to challenge their leaders at every level to be a leadership under God by governing with spiritual and moral values. Some will come together in parliamentary prayer fellowships to support one another and seek God's wisdom in policy making. People will be hungry for a relationship with God, and there will be spiritual revival. People's hearts and lives will be transformed.

Finally, you will know that a community is grasping the vision of reconciliation when they begin to become messengers themselves to others within their sphere of influence. In a sense, faith-based reconciliation is a holy cause, which needs passionate advocates. It leads to spiritual and social revolution, which needs revolutionaries. It is a prophetic movement that needs messengers to carry its dynamic message to all the nations.

A second item on the agenda is the building of bridges between communities, which mean developing the tangible and intangible strands of connectedness among diverse people groups so that they can live together in peace and seek the common good for the whole community. Bridge builders function as civic diplomats, moving quietly among diverse communities to build relationship, establish trust, and develop understanding.

How do you know that a bridge is actually being built between two communities? You must take a long-term strategic view if you do not want to be discouraged by lack of immediate results or setbacks. Bridge builders are often regarded with great suspicion, particularly by members of their own constituency or community. How can you have anything to do with "those people? How can you even give credibility to those people who have evil intentions? Be prepared to be misunderstood, considered naïve, criticized, or even verbally or physically assaulted. As a reconciler, you will experience persecution even from your own community. However, in the end you will see a growing number of people from estranged communities willing to "chance the arm" by taking the first step to reach out to "the other." In the twenty-first century, given the growing centrality of religion in domestic and international affairs, it will be important to build bridges among the different religious traditions and especially among the members of the Abrahamic family. Ecumenical and interfaith dialogues, while limited in terms of what can be achieved, are still a valuable beginning to a process of deeper reconciliation. This will be especially important between the Judeo-Christian West and the Islamic world. U.S. military chaplains can play an enhanced role as diplomats in the Islamic world, which values an integration of faith and politics. There is a need to have bridges built between people of faith and secular people both in the United States and Europe. Particularly in the United States, we see that there are profoundly different worldviews represented by "red states" and "blue states."

The third item on the agenda is racial healing, which involves the task of addressing historical wounds stemming from injustice in a community. This is particularly important in nations that have engaged in the practice of institutional slave trade: the United States, Europe, and the Arab nations. In the United States, this will be particularly important between Anglos and African Americans because of the history of slavery, Jim Crow, and institutionalized white privilege. It will also be important between Anglos and Native Americans because of the history of ethnic cleansing and broken promises. In the Southwest, this will be important between Anglos and Latinos because of the legacy of Manifest Destiny. An important question to consider is "What does racial healing look like?" First of all, Anglos will need to honestly face up to how they have benefited from a system of white privilege and how that can be changed to level the playing field. Conversations, painful conversations about race, and racism are needed in our social institutions: our schools, religious communities, and professional organizations. How can the pie be expanded so as to create value for people of color? How can Anglos open doors and create opportunity for African Americans? Secondly, it will require people of color to give up suffering as a badge of honor and to grapple with the emerging complexities of black identity so that it is not simply tied to liberal Democratic Party politics. Hence, if an African American chooses to become a conservative Republican, he will not be seen as an "Uncle Tom" or as having sold out his own people. Those reconcilers called to focus on racial healing will encounter many Anglos with the attitude "I'm not apologizing for anything. I didn't have anything to do with slavery!" They will also encounter African Americans with the attitude "I'm not forgiving anything because nothing will change." When you have reached this point in the conversation, you will know that you have touched the core of the wound.

A fourth item on the agenda is the task of healing the broken family of Abraham. Three great faith traditions—Jews, Christians, and Muslims— trace their spiritual roots back to Abraham and share in the Abrahamic tradition of submission to the one true God, the Abrahamic moral vision of faith-based reconciliation, and the Abrahamic mission of healing the nations. So much is shared among these spiritual cousins, and yet, over the centuries, there has been so much estrangement. In the post-September 11 environment, there is a desperate need for the children of Abraham to rediscover the Abrahamic moral vision and mission. In a time and context in which national security has become the operative paradigm in the affairs of nations, this is not a luxury. It is essential for our survival and for peace between nations. It is an embarrassing but well-established fact that each of the Abrahamic religious traditions bears responsibility for being a cause or contributor to conflict. At the same time, what is often overlooked is the tremendous spiritual capacity for peacemaking and reconciliation that is embedded in the sacred texts and in the principles and practices of Judaism, Christianity, and Islam.

So how do people of faith from the Abrahamic tradition recover our tradition, moral vision, and sacred mission? First, we must begin with healing the broken family of Abraham. Such a task will need to take into account the following realities:

- The Israeli/Palestinian conflict.
- The spirit of domination that exists in both the Judeo-Christian West and the Islamic world.

- The replacement theology wherein each part of the Abrahamic community views itself as the exclusive descendents of Abraham.
- The reemerging anti-Semitism in Europe and other parts of the world.
- The anti-Muslim attitudes in Europe, United States, and Africa.
- The unwillingness of Muslim-dominated states to share power with minority religious communities, such as Jews and Christians.
- The present U.S. foreign policy vision of American primacy.
- The present vision of global Jihad fostered by Saudi Wahabhism, Hizbut Tahrir (HT), the Muslim Brotherhood, and Al Qaeda.

I am encouraged by the growing number of people of faith with a call to the work of reconciliation that are addressing various aspects of healing the broken family of Abraham. Increasing numbers of Christians are exploring their Jewish roots. Abrahamic dialogues are becoming very popular in the United States. Amman-based institutes are seeking to promote Christian-Muslim dialogue and to engage in the battlefield of ideas about the true nature of Islam. However, I believe that in the years ahead, the single greatest challenge to agents of reconciliation will be to promote faith-based reconciliation as *the alternative* to religious extremism.

A fifth item on the agenda is peacemaking and conflict resolution, which needs faith-based practitioners who are able to integrate the best of conflict resolution methodology with the transcendent principles and practices of religious faith. Such skills as conflict analysis, negotiation, mediation, arbitration, and communication need to be augmented by prayer, fasting, sacred texts, spiritual conversations, sacred rituals of healing, forgiveness, and reconciliation. I would hope to see a growing number of people of faith embrace this noble discipline in all aspects of our society. I would hope to see the skills of conflict resolution taught as a standard part of our public school curriculum. I would hope to see apologies and forgiveness become an expected norm in social discourse and as a sign of individual character. I would hope to see conflict resolution become an indispensable skill in leadership training seminars. I would hope to see the establishment of a U.S. Academy for Reconciliation, which would welcome the faith-based dimension.

A sixth item on the agenda is advocacy for social justice, which involves taking action on behalf of an oppressed group in general or in relationship to a specific cause that requires action by the civic, state, or federal authorities. Usually, the task of advocacy places the advocate in an antagonistic role with the authorities or a privileged segment of society. Advocacy includes fasts, picketing, demonstrations, lobbying, and political organization. Advocacy involves changing unjust systems and structures that provide privilege for one group and disadvantage for others. I would hope to see Muslim advocates of social justice in the Islamic world increasingly serve as prophetic voices in their societies. Where are the prophetic voices in Saudi Arabia that challenge the exportation of Wahabi ideology to the Middle East, South Asia, North Africa, Europe, and the United States? I would hope to see Christian advocates of social justice in Europe, in the United States, and in Latin America. Where are the prophetic voices in Germany that challenge the isolation of Turkish Muslims in Berlin or the prophetic voices in the United States that challenge the treatment of law-abiding Muslims by homeland security officials? Where are the prophetic voices in Brazil that challenge a society that sees large and growing populations of workers in the municipal dumps recycling plastic? I would hope to see Jewish advocates of social justice in Israel, in the United States, and in Europe. Where are the prophetic voices in Israel that challenge the treatment of Palestinians, particularly the ever-diminishing Christian population on the West Bank and in Gaza.

A seventh item on the agenda is repairing the torn fabric of societies by fostering individual and collective forgiveness for past wounds. This healing process requires a transformation of hearts on the civil society and grass roots level. As has been pointed out in an earlier chapter, without political forgiveness, groups have no possibility of a future together. Of particular importance will be healing the wounds of the twentieth century, which will be an enormous task. The twentieth century began and ended with wars and was the bloodiest century in human history in terms of the number of deaths, violence, refugees, and displacement. This means that the twenty-first century promises to be the most dangerous of all, given the large number of unhealed communities that circle the globe.

An eighth item on the agenda is raising up leadership guided by spiritual and moral principles, which involves the task of promoting the transcendent dimensions of reconciliation by challenging both leaders and people to submit their lives to God. As has been pointed out in an earlier chapter, sovereignty is the dividing line between faith-based and secular forms of leadership. A faith-based person knows that apart from submission to God that communities cannot be completely healed. It is also important that the leadership of a community be guided by spiritual and moral principles and feel a sense of accountability to God for their actions. Who is bringing this challenge to heads of state, cabinet ministers, members of parliament, and military and national security leaders?

This also involves fostering spiritual renewal on the popular level by challenging people to find peace with God. Since reconciliation has both a vertical and horizontal dimension to it, the faith-based reconciler should look for opportunities to bring people to the decision point of submitting their lives to God.

The first step to becoming an instrument of reconciliation is to say yes to God. Our lives and our desires are shaped by defining moments. Defining moments consist of choices that we consciously make to respond to the call of God. Perhaps, this is one of those defining moments for you, where your heart is stirred by the vision of faith-based reconciliation; and you are asking yourself "What is the first step?" The first step is to say yes to God. However, are you prepared to say yes to God? Are you prepared to be transformed yourself? Are you willing to be used by God in whatever situations you are called? Let's consider some of the possible obstacles to a yes response. First would be obstacles of the heart. Perhaps, you have intellectual obstacles, such as a lack of knowledge or skills or objections to the message of reconciliation. Perhaps, you have emotional obstacles such as wounding, unforgiveness, or poor self-image that cause you to lack emotional strength to reach out to others. Perhaps you fear facing painful realities in your own life. Perhaps, you have volitional obstacles such as stubbornness in surrender to God or prejudice toward other people groups that cause you to actively resist the call to be a reconciler. Second would be obstacles of circumstance such as family problems, poor health of a spouse, and parental demands. There might be job, office, or career obstacles such as long demanding hours with little flexibility. There might be other obstacles such as financial pressure or debt. What obstacles, if any, are honestly holding you back from saying yes to God?

So the Abrahamic tradition, moral vision, and mission began as a promise to one person. God promised Abraham that he would be a blessing to all nations and that it would take on the form of *tikkun olam*—to heal, to repair, and to transform the world. Abraham had the courage to take that first step on a long journey. The baton of faith-based reconciliation has been passed by people of faith from one generation to another. And now, the baton is being passed to us in the fullness of time. Will our generation take up the baton and run the course? All the heavenly hosts are watching us.